MW01042745

INTRODUCTION

*Y*ou've probably heard a lot of people use the word *epic*. We often use it to say something or someone is awesome or spectacular. Whether it's epic fails, epic movies, or epic cookies, people use this word all the time. But is that all *epic* really means?

Epic is traditionally defined as a special kind of story that shares the deeds of a great hero or tells the history of a special people. When you're older, you'll probably read at least one of the great epics in literature class, but you don't have to wait to read the greatest epic ever written. You can read it right now. It's the Bible.

In the Bible, you'll read many stories about inspiring heroes: a young king slays a giant with a stone; a prophet calls down fire from heaven; an enemy of God's people becomes a great preacher. But these stories, and every story in the Bible, work together to tell one larger story—an amazing story that runs through every page of the Bible, from Genesis to Revelation. The true story of God's work to save the whole world from sin through the life, death, and resurrection of His Son, Jesus Christ—the great Hero of this epic.

That's why this book exists, and why we've called it *Epic*. We want to introduce you to this incredible story God tells in the Bible so you can see how all the pieces fit together and keep sharing this great tale: the true story that began "in the beginning" and continues until the day all things are made new.

CONTENTS

THE **STORY** THAT CHANGED THE WORLD

EPIC

B&H
PUBLISHING GROUP
Nashville, Tennessee

RETOLD BY AARON ARMSTRONG
ILLUSTRATED BY HEATH MCPHERSON

Copyright © 2019 by B&H Publishing Group
All rights reserved.
978-1-5359-3812-9
Published by B&H Publishing Group,
Nashville, Tennessee
All Scripture quotations are taken from the Christian
Standard Bible®, Copyright © 2017 by Holman Bible Publishers.
Used by permission. Christian Standard Bible® and CSB® are
federally registered trademarks of Holman Bible Publishers.
DEWEY: J220.95 SBHD: BIBLE STORIES
Printed in December 2018 in Shenzhen, Guangdong, China
1 2 3 4 5 6 · 23 22 21 20 19

FOR MORE RESOURCES
TO HELP PEOPLE OF ALL AGES
EXPLORE THE BIBLE'S BIG STORY,
VISIT GOSPELPROJECT.COM

5

IN THE BEGINNING

What's the best kind of story?

Is it one filled with action and adventure? Is it one with drama and romance? One that makes you laugh or cry—or even both at the same time?

The world is filled with amazing stories—stories of hope and adventure and wonder. Stories that begin, "Once upon a time," "It was a dark and stormy night," and even, "A long time ago in a galaxy far, far away . . .". Stories where heroes slay dragons, the helpless find hope, and enemies are defeated.

As amazing as these stories are, they pale in comparison to the greatest story, the one they all echo—the story that is better than any of these stories because it is true. The story that gives God the most glory.

The one that begins, "In the beginning . . ."

Before the beginning, there was nothing—no sun, no moon, no stars, no *anything*.

Almost.

There was one thing; not a thing really, but a Person: *God*, the One who has no beginning and no end, who always was and always will be, who needs nothing because He has everything He needs in Himself.

In the beginning, God created the heavens and the earth in the most amazing way possible, in the way that would bring Himself the most glory: through His word.

When He first formed the world, there was nothing but darkness and water, so God spoke as His Spirit hovered over the water . . .

LET THERE BE LIGHT!

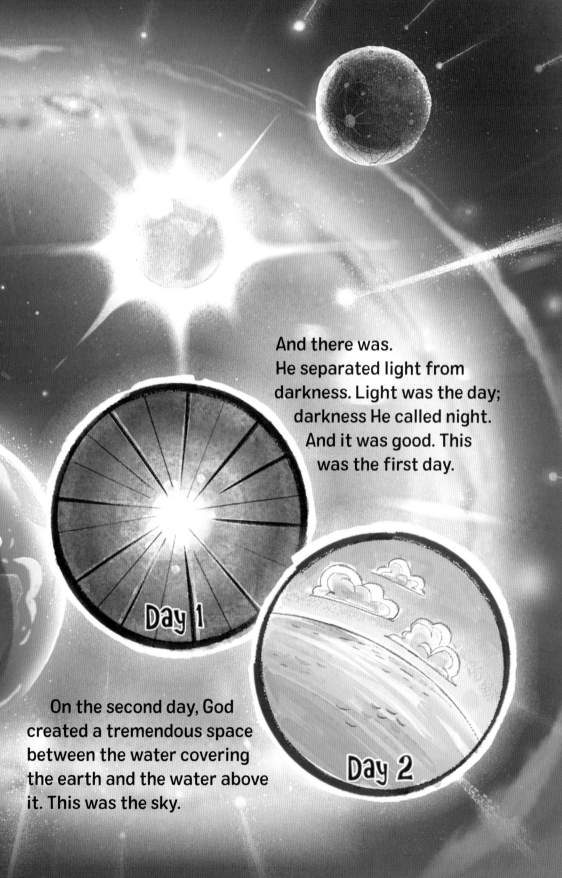

And there was.
He separated light from
darkness. Light was the day;
darkness He called night.
And it was good. This
was the first day.

Day 1

Day 2

On the second day, God
created a tremendous space
between the water covering
the earth and the water above
it. This was the sky.

On the third day, God separated the dry land from the water, dividing earth and sea. Then He called for plants and trees to grow from the earth—plants that were beautiful, filled with fruit and seeds that would be good to eat.

On the fourth day, God said that two lights should shine in the sky: the sun for the day and the moon for the night. He made the stars too.

On the fifth day, God began to make living creatures! Fish and other sea life swam in the waters of the earth. Birds soared through the sky.

On the sixth day, God made even more creatures—livestock, wildlife, and crawling creatures—to fill the earth.

Every day as He looked at what He had made, He declared that it was good. And it was. Everything was wonderful. Everything was perfect. It was a world designed to glorify Him in every way.

But God wasn't done yet.

As He looked at all He had made, God said, "Let us make man in Our image." And He did. But instead of simply speaking mankind into existence, God chose to create man in the way that would bring Him the most glory.

God formed a body in the dirt, lovingly shaping and designing it with His hands, delighting in this next creative act. He breathed into the body, giving it life, and the body opened its eyes, alive—Adam, the first human being.

An image bearer, unique among all God's creatures, was given the responsibility of protecting and caring for all that God had made, to be God's representative in the world.

IT IS GOOD!

He placed the man in a garden, Eden, where every kind of plant and tree grew. It was Adam's home—the place where he and his Creator would walk together. Two special trees stood in the garden: the tree of life and the tree of the knowledge of good and evil.

"You are free to eat from any tree of this garden," God said, "but you must not eat from the tree of the knowledge of good and evil, for on the day you eat from it, you will certainly die."

Then as He looked at all He had made, for the first time, God said, *"This is not good."*

What was not good? All that He had made was perfect. All that existed was exactly as God intended, including His image bearer, . . . but something was missing: the man was alone.

IT IS NOT GOOD FOR THE MAN TO BE ALONE.

There was no other like him in all creation, so God determined to make him a helper, another image bearer, equal in every way to the man. Once again, God did something unique, creating this new being in the way that would give Him the most glory. Instead of speaking the second image bearer into existence, instead of forming this one from the dust of the earth as He did with the man, God formed this helper *from* the man as he slept.

When he awoke and saw his companion for the first time, the man was delighted. She was the perfect helper for him— the one who was his equal, his wife, the first woman.

God blessed them, and gave them authority over all the earth. They were to rule over it, to care for and cultivate it, a calling passed down from them to their children, and to every generation of humanity.

Finally, everything was good. Everything was perfect, exactly as God had intended, and so, as the first humans rejoiced together in the garden, God said, "It is *very* good."

On the seventh day, God rested. The work of creation was finished in the way that would bring God the most glory, because that's what this story is really about. It's the true story of how God is glorified—not only in how He made the world, but how He shows that He loves it. He spoke the world into existence, spoke to His image bearers in the garden, and gave His Word to their descendants.

Thousands of years later, He would do something even greater: He would send a person into the world who *was* the Word of God. This Word would live among human beings as one of them. He would show them how deeply God loves them, and He would show it most completely by putting right what was about to go wrong.

HOW CAN WE GLORIFY GOD AS WE INTERACT WITH THE WORLD AROUND US?

THE DAY EVERYTHING WENT WRONG

God made the world and everything in it to be perfect, wonderful, and just as it should be. Then the first humans ruined everything. In the garden were two special trees, one of which was the tree of the knowledge of good and evil. God had placed only one restriction on His image bearers: They were forbidden from eating the fruit of this tree. They were welcome to eat of any other tree, just not *this* one, because when they did, they would certainly die.

In the garden, there was a serpent, the most cunning of all the wild animals. And it could speak. It wanted to test these creatures who were like God, to see if they would betray their Creator's command. So it set to work and approached the woman with a seemingly innocent question.

> Did God **really** say, "You can't eat from any tree in the garden"?

> We can eat the fruit from all the trees in the garden, except this one. God said, "You must not eat it or touch it, or you will die."

> No! You will not die. In fact, God knows that when you eat it your eyes will be opened and you will be like God.

Like God? Aren't we already like Him? Aren't we made in His image? Questions flooded Eve's mind, doubts about God's character and His goodness. Perhaps He really was holding back something good from them after all.

She looked at the tree again, and this time, she did not see it as a tree not to be eaten from or even touched. She saw an opportunity. It's fruit was delightful to look at and could help her and Adam gain wisdom. So she reached out, took a piece of the fruit . . . and ate it. Then she gave it to her husband, who was next to her the entire time, saying nothing. He ate it too.

It was delicious. It was everything they hoped for, like the greatest thing you've ever eaten, only better still. Until it wasn't.

Their eyes opened, and for the first time, they saw that they were naked! And they felt something new. Something they were never meant to feel. Something ugly and foreign. *Shame.*

They hid themselves from one another, covering themselves with fig leaves.

Then they heard Him. God had come walking in the garden. Surely He must know what had happened! They remembered God's warning: when they ate of the fruit of that tree, they would certainly die. They hid among the trees, their shame complete. Not only were they hiding from one another, but they were hiding from their Creator. The One they were made to reflect in creation.

"Where are you?" God called to the man.

The man called from his hiding place, "I heard You in the garden, and I was afraid because I was naked, so I hid."

DID YOU EAT FROM THE TREE THAT I COMMANDED YOU NOT TO EAT FROM?

The woman **You** gave to be with me—she gave me some fruit.

The serpent deceived me!

God knew what would happen when they ate from that tree. They had welcomed death into the world. The perfect relationship the man and woman enjoyed had been ruined, their trust of one another replaced with blame-shifting and pain.

Work became difficult, and food would only be grown through much toil and struggle. They would eat by the sweat of their brow.

And, eventually but certainly, they would die.

Worst of all, the man and woman could no longer be with their Creator in the garden. He could not allow them to eat from the tree of life with this curse upon them. So He cast them out and placed an angel with a fiery sword at the garden's gate to prevent them from returning.

But before He did all this, He gave them a message of hope, a promise: Despite their sin, they would not die immediately. Instead, the woman was given a name: Eve, "the mother of all the living." They would have children, and their children would have children, and then their children would have children as well. And someday, one of their children would battle the serpent. The serpent would injure Him, but He would crush its head.

Adam and Eve left the garden broken and ashamed, but also with hope. The serpent would pay for what it had done. The deceiver would die, and God's image bearers would be restored.

Away from the garden, Adam and Eve had a son, Cain. When he was born, they were filled with excitement—they had a baby, a son! They remembered the promise God gave them, that one of their children would crush the head of the serpent and redeem them.

Then they had another son, Abel, and more children followed.

When Cain and Abel had grown, they offered sacrifices to the Lord. Cain, a farmer, brought some of the produce of the land; Abel, a shepherd, brought the first-born of his flock. God was pleased with Abel's sacrifice, but paid no attention to Cain's. Cain was furious. How could God prefer Abel's offering to his own? But the issue wasn't with his offering—it was

his heart. Cain didn't believe. He lacked faith. God spoke to him, encouraging him to put away his anger. Sin, He said, was crouching at the door, waiting to devour him. *But Cain did not listen.*

Instead, Cain called Abel to the field, and there Cain attacked his brother and killed him. In that moment, the world's first child became its first murderer. The one his parents may have secretly hoped would be the one to crush the serpent only crushed his brother.

HOW CAN YOU PROTECT YOURSELF AGAINST DOUBTING WHAT GOD HAS SAID?

Although all hope seemed lost, God's promise would not be stopped. Adam and Eve had another son, Seth, and from his family would come another Son, One who would crush the serpent and give up His life to put right all that had gone wrong.

A WARNING, A FLOOD, AND A PROMISE

Wherever Adam and Eve's family went, wickedness and evil followed. It was all they wanted to do; their only desire was "nothing but evil all the time"—to live in defiance of their Creator, the One in whose image they were made. So great was their sin that God, regretting ever having made humanity, decided to wipe them from the face of the earth.

I WILL WIPE MANKIND OFF THE FACE OF THE EARTH—FOR I REGRET THAT I MADE THEM.

God looked down upon His creation, and He grieved. All humanity was condemned. None would be spared. Except for Noah—the one who walked with God, who found favor in the eyes of the Lord—and his family.

I AM BRINGING A FLOOD TO DESTROY EVERY CREATURE UNDER HEAVEN WITH THE BREATH OF LIFE IN IT. EVERYTHING ON EARTH WILL PERISH.

BRING WITH YOU TWO OF ALL THE LIVING CREATURES SO THAT YOU CAN KEEP THEM ALIVE.

Noah did everything that God commanded. For one hundred years, Noah built the massive ark—the ship that would offer salvation from the coming flood. As he worked, he warned all around him of God's coming judgment.

They did not listen. They did not care.

And then, the rain began.

A single drop. Then another. And another. The water burst forth from below the earth, even as it poured down from the sky above.

For forty days, the flood raged. The waters covered everything, even the tops of the mountains. Nothing that walked on the surface of the earth survived. Nothing except those who had been spared on the ark. Two of every kind of creature, and eight humans. Noah and his family—the one who found favor in the sight of God.

For 150 days after the rain ceased, the flood remained on the earth.

Slowly, the water began to go down, and seven months after the flood began, the ark came to rest among the mountains of Ararat. Soon, the tops of the mountains could be seen again.

Noah opened a window for the first time since God Himself had sealed them in before the flood began. Noah sent out a raven from the ark to see if the waters had dried. It did not return. Then he sent a dove, but it found nowhere dry and clean to rest, so it returned. Seven days later, Noah sent it out again. This time, it returned with a plucked olive leaf in its beak. After another seven days, Noah sent the dove out yet again, but this time, it did not return. The flood was over. It was time to leave the ark.

Noah built an altar to the Lord and made an offering that pleased Him. Then God blessed Noah and his family, calling them to have many children—to rebuild the human race. God once again gave them authority over all creation.

Then God made a covenant (or promise) with Noah and all who would come after him, swearing that He would never again send a flood to destroy the earth. As a sign of the covenant, He created a rainbow that would appear in the clouds.

But the flood didn't end humanity's sin problem. Sin continued in the hearts of Noah and his descendants, growing steadily as humans looked for ways to make a name for themselves—whether by building towers to their own achievement or declaring themselves gods.

And through it all, God kept His word. Despite their sin, humans were not wiped off the face of the earth. Instead, God prepared the way for a permanent solution to sin: the Son promised to Adam and Eve would finally arrive to defeat the serpent. He would be the way of salvation for all and show favor to everyone who believes in Him.

God began this task by speaking to a man named Abram.

SIN DESERVES PUNISHMENT, BUT GOD CONTINUES TO BE PATIENT WITH US. HOW CAN WE RESPOND TO GOD'S KINDNESS?

THE PROMISE AND BLESSING

Abram could hardly believe what he was hearing. The Lord had spoken to him and said that all the people of the earth would be blessed through him! *Him*—Abram. A seventy-five-year-old man with no children. No heir. No one to carry on his legacy or family name. How could *he* be a blessing to anyone?

He didn't know, but God told him, "I will make your offspring like the dust of the earth, so that if anyone could count the dust of the earth, then your offspring could be counted."

Abram and his wife, Sarai, would have a child and many descendants. Was this possible? Abram couldn't see how, but he believed.

Time passed. Abram still had no offspring, no heir of his own. But God appeared to him and repeated the promise: "Look at the sky and count the stars, if you are able to. Your offspring will be that numerous."

God also promised that all the land he could see would belong to Abram and his family. Abram believed, but asked, "How will I know this will happen?"

38

God commanded Abram to bring animals for a sacrifice, but this was no ordinary sacrifice. This sacrifice was meant to seal a *covenant*, a binding promise between God and Abram.

As darkness fell, God caused a deep sleep to fall over Abram. Then He told him of what was to come.

Abram would die at a good old age, surrounded by his loved ones. Abram's descendants would live in a land not their own, as slaves; but God's people would be freed and would return to the promised land at just the right time—the time God had appointed to judge the inhabitants of the land.

Then, as Abram slept, God gave a sign of His vow: a smoking fire pot and a fiery torch appeared and passed through the sacrifice.

The covenant was made; the oath was sworn, and only God was responsible for it. He would keep His promise to bless Abram and make a great nation of His descendants no matter what. Even if Abram's faith faltered, God's promise would not fail.

And Abram *did* falter. He had a son, a boy named Ishmael. But Sarai was not his mother, and Ishmael was not the promised child. But God swore again that Abram would be the father of great nations and have offspring as numerous as the stars. He gave Abram a sign of this covenant and a new name, Abraham. He renamed Sarai as well, calling her Sarah. But He was clear: Ishmael was not the heir, the child of the promise. That child would come, but they must wait.

Years passed. Abraham was ninety-nine, and the promised child still had not come. Then one day three men came to his tents, and the Lord was among them. Abraham and Sarah prepared a meal for their guests. As they ate, the Lord spoke:

"I will certainly come back to you in about a year's time, and your wife Sarah will have a son!"

Abraham was in shock, but he believed. Sarah, listening from her tent, laughed. *Really? Now?* She was an old woman—far too old to be a mother. She couldn't believe it was possible.

Even so, God's promise was greater than her unbelief. Soon she discovered she was expecting a baby, and a year later, she was holding her son, Isaac, the long-promised child, the one through whom God would bless all the nations. Through Isaac's descendants would come *another* child who had been promised long before, in the garden. He would be the offspring who would crush the head of the serpent, the One who would rescue God's people from the curse of sin forevermore.

WAITING FOR GOD TO FULFILL HIS PROMISES CAN BE DIFFICULT FOR US. WHAT CAN WE DO TO KEEP TRUSTING AND NOT LOSE HOPE?

THE SON, THE RAM, AND THE SACRIFICE

> *Wait here for the boy and me to return to you.*

Questions raced through Abraham's mind as he walked, Isaac and his servant beside him. *How could the Lord ask this? How could He want me to sacrifice my son, the child God Himself had promised would be born? What will happen to the promise—the covenant sworn all those years ago?*

But he trusted God. *Surely, since He was faithful to fulfill the promise of a son, He will be faithful to the promise of my offspring being as numerous as the stars in the sky.* So he trusted and walked on.

They reached the mountain, the one God had told him about. Abraham turned to his servant and told him to wait for his return. Then the father and son climbed the mountain. The son carried the wood on his back. The father carried the knife and his fears.

How could God ask me to sacrifice my son? he wondered. He didn't know. He couldn't know. But he knew his God. And so he trusted. *The Lord will provide the sacrifice*, he thought. As he built the altar, trying and failing to hold back tears, he continued to tell himself the truth. *The Lord will provide—He has to provide.*

Then Isaac spoke. "Where is the sacrifice?"

"The Lord will provide," he said, so softly it was barely a whisper.

He knew the words were true: Abraham trusted that God would provide the sacrifice. He just didn't know how it would happen.

Abraham tied up his son and placed him on the altar.

He raised the knife in his unsteady hand, ready to follow God's command, even as he trusted God would spare his son.

God will provide, he thought, taking a weak, quivering breath before the plunging blow. *The Lord will fulfill His promise.*

ABRAHAM! ABRAHAM! DO NOT HARM THE BOY.

NOW I KNOW THAT YOU FEAR GOD, BECAUSE YOU HAVE NOT HELD BACK YOUR SON FROM ME.

The knife fell from Abraham's hand. Abraham fell to his knees, overcome with relief. His tears of anguish turning to tears of joy.

At that moment, Abraham heard something rustling in a nearby thicket. God had provided the offering, a ram, caught by its horns, a substitute for Isaac, his promised son. As the offering burned on the altar, the Lord spoke again, declaring that because Abraham obeyed God, He would indeed bless him.

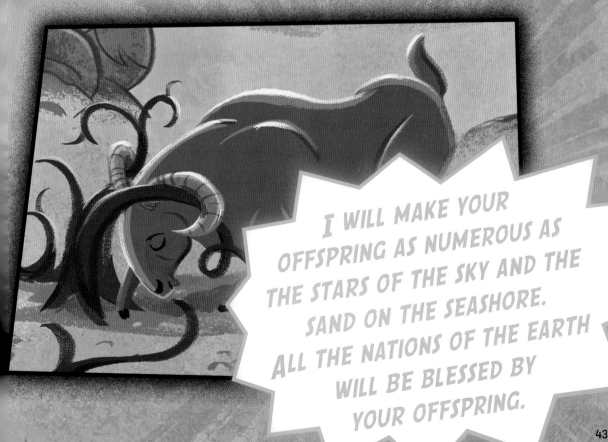

I WILL MAKE YOUR OFFSPRING AS NUMEROUS AS THE STARS OF THE SKY AND THE SAND ON THE SEASHORE. ALL THE NATIONS OF THE EARTH WILL BE BLESSED BY YOUR OFFSPRING.

As Abraham and Isaac returned from the mountain, Abraham's heart was full of joy. His son had been spared. A substitute had been provided. Abraham believed, and His faith was not in vain.

God continued to be faithful to Abraham all the years of his life. After Sarah died, Abraham sent a servant to his own people to find a wife for Isaac. After making the journey to Abraham's homeland, the servant prayed that the Lord would lead him to the right woman with a sign: that the woman who would marry Isaac would give water to his camels.

Before he had even finished praying, Rebekah arrived and gave water to the servant's camels. He rejoiced and asked her about her family. She was a relative of Abraham and Isaac. *This is the one*, he thought, and he praised God. Then he went to her family and asked for their blessing to bring her back to Abraham's home. They agreed, and she went with him. When she arrived, Rebekah became Isaac's wife.

Abraham died, old and content, having lived a long life. Although he did not live to see the promise of many descendants fulfilled—or the promise of a descendant who would bless all the earth—he died trusting that God would fulfill it.

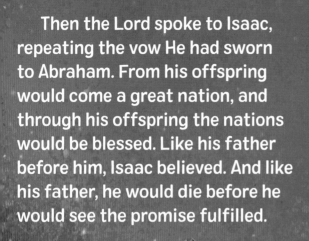

Then the Lord spoke to Isaac, repeating the vow He had sworn to Abraham. From his offspring would come a great nation, and through his offspring the nations would be blessed. Like his father before him, Isaac believed. And like his father, he would die before he would see the promise fulfilled.

But we know God *did* keep His word. The promise passed from Abraham to Isaac, and then to one of Isaac's sons, and then to his children, and on and on through the ages, until one day another Son appeared: God's only Son, who would carry the wood upon which He would be sacrificed, to a mountain where his life would not be spared—because He was the true sacrifice. A Son whose life and death would bless all the nations.

GOD WANTS US TO BE CONFIDENT THAT HE WILL KEEP HIS PROMISES. HOW CAN YOU REMIND YOURSELF THAT GOD IS FAITHFUL TO DO WHAT HE SAYS IN HIS WORD?

Genesis 25–36

GOD'S KINDNESS TO A SCHEMER

Jacob was jerked awake as a Man grabbed him. The two began to wrestle. Though this Stranger was powerful, Jacob would not yield. Not until he received His blessing.

This was the theme of Jacob's early life. All his life, Jacob had been fighting, scheming, and chasing after a blessing—one that was his all along. Before he was even born, he and his twin brother, Esau, wrestled in the womb, and when he was born, he was grasping Esau's heel. Hence his name: Jacob. The heel-grabber. Deceiver. Schemer.

As the boys grew, their father, Isaac, favored Esau, who loved to hunt and fish. Jacob, the younger, was quiet and crafty, and preferred to stay in the tents with his mother. Jacob used his craftiness to his advantage at every opportunity.

One day Esau returned from the field exhausted, and he demanded some of the stew Jacob was making.

"First sell me your birthright."

Esau's birthright, his inheritance and status in the family, was far more valuable than a bowl of stew, and Jacob knew it. But Esau didn't care. All that concerned him in that moment was his hunger. He swore that his birthright belonged to Jacob. Before long, his hunger had been replaced by bitterness toward his brother. But Jacob was not done scheming yet. Esau still had something far more valuable than his birthright. He had his father's blessing.

When Isaac was an old man and unable to see, Jacob made his move.

He came to his father dressed in his brother's clothing and wearing sheep skins to cover his arms (Esau was much hairier than him). Isaac called him over, smelling his clothes— Esau's clothes—and blessed his son.

> Ah, the smell of my son
> is like the smell of a field
> that the Lord has blessed.
>
> May God give to you—
> from the dew of the sky
> and from the richness of
>   the land—
> an abundance of grain
>   and new wine.
>
> May peoples serve you
> and nations bow in
>   worship to you.
> Be master over your
>   relatives;
> may your mother's sons
>   bow in worship to you.
> Those who curse you will
>   be cursed,
> and those who bless you
>   will be blessed.

Then Jacob left, having stolen Esau's blessing.

When Isaac and Esau learned of Jacob's betrayal, both men were furious. After pleading for another blessing, Esau stormed out of the tents, determined to kill his brother as soon as their father died. But Jacob fled to the land of Ur, the land of their ancestors, to stay with his uncle, Laban.

As Jacob traveled, he found himself in the presence of God, who promised that Jacob would be blessed with descendants too numerous to count and that all the nations would be blessed through his offspring. It was the same promise God made to his father and to his grandfather before him.

The promise was always Jacob's, before his striving against his brother began. The promise would change the entire world.

But first, God would humble the schemer.

Jacob fell in love with Rachel the moment he laid eyes on her. He asked her father and his uncle, Laban, for his permission to marry her, and offered to work for seven years for her. Laban agreed and arranged the wedding . . . but with his other daughter, Leah, as the bride.

When Jacob realized he'd been tricked, he confronted Laban, who explained that it was against their customs for the younger to be married first. But, he said, Jacob could marry Rachel too—if he worked for another seven years. Jacob agreed, married Rachel and got to work.

Years passed. Jacob's family grew as both Rachel and Leah had children. Laban and Jacob's rivalry grew as well. Throughout the twenty years Jacob worked for him, Laban changed Jacob's wages ten times, always in an attempt to gain the upper hand over his son-in-law. Finally, Jacob left to return to Canaan, taking his family and all his possessions with him.

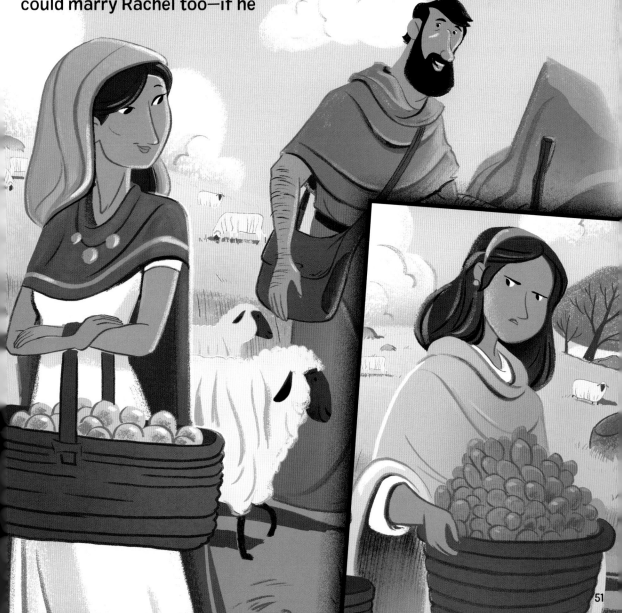

Returning home meant facing Esau, the brother he had cheated of both birthright and blessing. The brother who had vowed to kill him so many years ago.

But first, he would face another opponent. The Man who appeared in the night and began to wrestle with him until daybreak. All through the night, they fought, but Jacob would not yield. Finally in the early morning hours, the Man struck Jacob's hip and dislocated it. But Jacob would still not loosen his grip. Not until the Man blessed him.

"What is your name?" The Man said.

"Jacob," he replied.

"It will be Israel because you have struggled with God and with men and have prevailed."

The Man blessed him, and then was gone. Jacob—Israel— was alone. The Man, he realized was no mere human being. He had seen God face-to-face and been spared. He walked with a limp for the rest of his days, a reminder of God's mercy to him.

Jacob had tried to win God's blessing in the same way he had plotted to gain his father's blessing. But there was no way to win or scheme his way to this blessing. It was a blessing he didn't deserve, but it was one that was freely given, because God had always intended to give it to him. The blessing led to the blessing of all the people of the earth as his descendents became as numerous as the dust of the earth and the stars in the sky. A great nation through which would come a greater blessing—a descendent of Jacob, a member of the family of Israel, who was no mere human being: Jesus, the Man who was God, who would give His life to bless all who would believe.

HOW DOES IT CHANGE THE WAY WE LIVE TO KNOW GOD'S BLESSING IS NOT SOMETHING WE CAN EARN, BUT THAT HE FREELY BLESSES ALL WHO TRUST IN CHRIST?

GOD USES EVIL FOR GOOD

*L*isten to this dream I had."

Those words would seal Joseph's fate—and spare the lives of his family. He just didn't know it yet.

Joseph was the most favored of all Jacob's children. He was the one who got the best of everything, including a very expensive robe of many colors. Now he was having dreams, visions, delusions of grandeur. They would all be bowing down to him—even their father. *Yeah right,* his brothers may have thought. *Let's do something about this dreamer.*

WE NEED TO DO SOMETHING ABOUT THIS DREAMER.

PLEASE HELP ME, BROTHERS!

His brothers agreed that they would kill him—except Reuben, the oldest, who said they should throw him down a well instead. Reuben left after his brothers agreed to his plan (he secretly planned to come back and rescue Joseph later).

The remaining brothers called for Joseph to join them. When he arrived, they beat him, took his robe, and threw him into the well. They sat down to eat a meal, and looked up to see slave traders traveling by. The brothers called to the men and sold Joseph.

All the while, God was using their betrayal for their good. They just didn't know it yet.

Joseph was taken to Egypt and sold to a man named Potiphar. There, God blessed him, giving him favor with his master and authority over all Potiphar owned. Potiphar's wife also liked Joseph, but she liked him in a romantic way. She attempted to convince Joseph to betray his master. He refused, running from her, but he left behind his cloak. She then lied about Joseph and said he had attacked her. Enraged, Potiphar threw Joseph into prison.

This is the dream...

There Joseph met two fellow prisoners, a baker and a cup-bearer. Both had been in the service of Pharaoh and both had dreamed strange dreams they couldn't understand. They told Joseph their dreams.

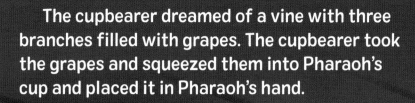

The cupbearer dreamed of a vine with three branches filled with grapes. The cupbearer took the grapes and squeezed them into Pharaoh's cup and placed it in Pharaoh's hand.

"This is the meaning," Joseph said: "In three days, you will be restored to your position serving Pharaoh. When this happens, tell him what has happened to me—how I am a Hebrew who was kidnapped and have done nothing to deserve being in this prison."

The baker told Joseph his dream: three baskets of white bread sat on his head. The baked goods were for Pharaoh, but birds ate them out of the baskets.

Joseph turned to the baker: "In three days you will be executed, hung from a tree, and your head will be removed. Birds will eat your body."

On the third day, these events came to pass. The baker was hanged, and the cupbearer was restored to his position. The cupbearer forgot about Joseph. But God was using this for the good of Joseph's family. Joseph just didn't know it yet.

Two years later, Pharaoh was plagued by strange dreams: Seven well-fed cows were eaten by seven sickly ones, and seven plump heads of grain were swallowed by seven withered ones. No one could interpret the dreams for him. None of the magicians or wise men could understand them. Then the cupbearer remembered the prisoner who could interpret dreams.

Joseph was brought from the prison to Pharaoh's court and was told the dreams. Joseph explained that the dreams were actually the same: there would be seven years of great harvest in the land of Egypt, but they would be followed by seven years of great famine that would devastate the land.

But Joseph didn't stop at explaining the dream. He offered a solution.

Take a fifth of the harvest during the seven years of abundance and store it as a food reserve for the seven years of famine. Then the country will not be wiped out by the famine.

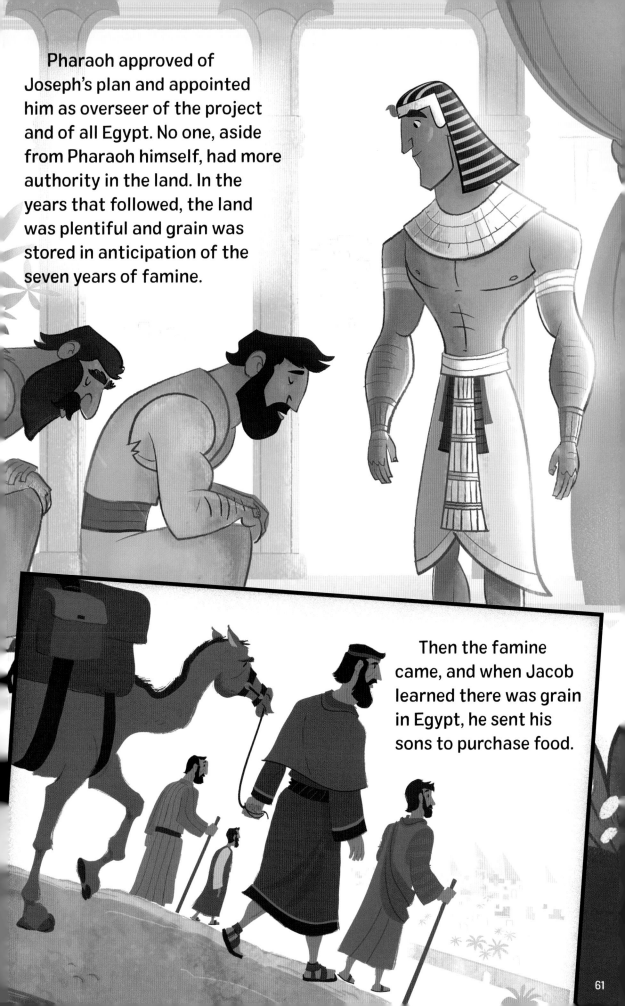

Pharaoh approved of Joseph's plan and appointed him as overseer of the project and of all Egypt. No one, aside from Pharaoh himself, had more authority in the land. In the years that followed, the land was plentiful and grain was stored in anticipation of the seven years of famine.

Then the famine came, and when Jacob learned there was grain in Egypt, he sent his sons to purchase food.

They arrived and bowed before Pharaoh's overseer, the man who sold grain to all who traveled to the country—their brother, Joseph.

They didn't recognize him, but the brother they'd sold into slavery years before was standing before them, the one they had convinced their father was dead. But Joseph knew them. And he saw an opportunity... but for what? To pay them back for their treachery? To be restored to his father? Or, perhaps, to bless them? First, Joseph would test them.

Joseph insisted they were spies and sent them away with a test: if they were honest, they could leave to relieve the hunger of their households. But one of the brothers had to stay behind. The remaining brothers were forbidden from returning unless they brought their youngest brother with them.

Reuben said, "See? Didn't I tell you not to harm Joseph? Now we are going to pay for what we have done!"

Joseph took Simeon and bound him. He sent the others away, grain in hand. As they ate and saw their store of grain was getting smaller with each day, they began to worry. What would happen if they went back to Egypt without Benjamin, the youngest of the brothers? Would they be declared spies and be imprisoned? Would something worse happen? And what would happen to Simeon if they didn't go back at all? So they waited, uncertain of what to do.

Then the food ran out. Jacob asked his sons to return to Egypt for more. The brothers warned their father that they couldn't return without Benjamin. Jacob, still heartbroken at the loss of Joseph, couldn't bear the thought of losing Benjamin as well.

We can't go back without Benjamin!

Why have you caused me so much trouble? Why did you tell the man that you had another brother?

Then Judah, Jacob's fourth son, stepped forward and made a vow with his father.

Send him with me. I will be responsible for him. But we should go—if we had not waited, we could have been there and back twice already!

The brothers left for Egypt. When they arrived, they stood before Joseph, who commanded they be brought to his home for a feast. They ate and drank together, and Benjamin received a larger portion than any of the others.

Then Joseph put them to one final test. He commanded his servants to place his silver cup in Benjamin's bags. When the brothers had left, Joseph told his servant to accuse them of theft.

The servant went out after the brothers and accused them. The brothers were in shock—none of them had stolen anything. But each allowed the servant to search his bags. When he found the silver cup in Benjamin's, they all cried out and tore their clothes to express their heartbreak. Then they loaded up their donkeys and returned to Joseph's house.

When they arrived, Joseph declared that the others were free to go, but Benjamin must stay behind as his slave. But Judah was unwilling to lose his youngest brother and cause his father more pain. He explained how his father, Jacob, had been overwhelmed by the loss of Joseph and could not bear to lose another favorite son—it would kill him. Judah begged to be taken in Benjamin's place, offering his life for his brother's.

The one who did this will be My slave!

Please, take me instead! Our father has already lost one son; he cannot bear to lose another. His grief would overwhelm him!

Hearing his brother's plea, Joseph ordered his servants to leave the room. Tears began to stream down his face. He could test his brothers no longer. He revealed his true identity.

I am your brother Joseph, the one you sold into slavery!

The brothers were terrified. Their brother Joseph was the ruler of Egypt. What would he do to them? But Joseph saw the worry in their eyes, and told them God had used their evil act for good.

Joseph's brothers returned to their father, their bags filled with food and supplies and their hearts filled with joy. They told him Joseph was still alive and living as the ruler of Egypt. When Jacob saw his son alive—the son he had lost so many years before—he rejoiced. The son who was dead was alive again!

When Pharaoh learned of the existence of his most trusted servant's family, he encouraged them all to come to Egypt to be with Joseph. Jacob and all his descendants—his children and grandchildren—moved to the land of Goshen in Egypt, and his family was reunited.

Do not fear— what you intended for evil, God used for good.

Years later, before Jacob died, he blessed each of his sons and said one of them would rule over all the others forever. But this was not Joseph, his beloved son; it was *Judah*, the one who offered his life for Benjamin's. It was Judah's family that would grow into a powerful tribe from which would come a great King. A King whose heart would long for the Lord. A King from whom would come another King, One who would experience great evil at the hands of His brothers, even as He offered His life as a ransom for many. One from whose sacrifice would come the greatest good of all—the deliverance of His people.

HOW CAN WE TRUST THAT GOD WILL BRING GOOD FROM EVIL?

GOD SENDS A MEDIATOR

"LET MY PEOPLE GO!"

For four hundred years, Jacob's family—the people of Israel—had lived in Egypt. They first came as honored guests, but now they were slaves. The Pharaoh didn't know of Joseph and his faithful service to Egypt centuries earlier. All he saw was the size of the Hebrew community. *We need to deal with them,* he thought. *Otherwise when war breaks out they will join our enemies, fight against us, and leave.*

Pharaoh put overseers in charge of the Israelites, and the overseers treated them cruelly. Jacob's descendants were commanded to make bricks and build cities. When their numbers kept growing, Pharaoh commanded that their sons be put to death. Life was difficult for the Hebrews. They needed rescue and cried out for help.

God heard their cries.

When Moses was born, his mother hid him from Pharaoh's soldiers. When she could hide him no longer, she put him in a basket in the Nile River, where he floated to Pharaoh's daughter, who adopted him. He grew up in Pharaoh's home as a prince of Egypt.

But Moses did not stay a prince in Egypt. He fled the land after he killed a guard who had been mistreating one of the Hebrews. For forty years, he hid in Midian as a shepherd, married to the daughter of Jethro the priest, never intending to set foot in Egypt again.

Until he saw it—a bush near Horeb, the mountain of God, burning but not consumed by the fire. And a voice:

MOSES.
Here I am.
I AM THE GOD OF YOUR FATHER, THE GOD OF ABRAHAM, THE GOD OF ISAAC, AND THE GOD OF JACOB.

GO TO PHARAOH AND TELL HIM THAT THE LORD SAYS, "LET MY PEOPLE GO."
BUT KNOW THAT HE WILL NOT LISTEN. I WILL STRETCH OUT MY HAND
AND STRIKE EGYPT WITH ALL MY MIRACLES.
AFTER THAT, HE WILL LET YOU GO.

God sent Moses and his brother Aaron with him. Each time they appeared before Pharaoh, they said, "The Lord says, 'Let My people go.'"
But Pharaoh would not listen.
God sent a series of plagues—

TURNING WATER TO BLOOD,

FILLING THE LAND WITH FROGS, GNATS, AND SWARMS OF FLIES,

KILLING THEIR LIVESTOCK,

COVERING THEIR SKIN WITH BOILS,

DESTROYING THEIR CROPS WITH HAIL,

SENDING LOCUSTS TO EAT WHAT CROPS REMAINED,

AND COVERING THE LAND WITH DARKNESS.

After each plague, God gave Pharaoh an opportunity to repent, to let God's people go. But Pharaoh would not. His heart was hard and proud.

So God sent one final plague.

The Hebrews made sacrifices and painted their doorposts. They ate a meal of roast lamb and unleavened bread, and they waited to see what God would do.

Then they heard it. A cry. Then another. And another. And then another still until all they could hear was the wailing of all the houses where death had not passed over. Including Pharaoh's.

"Leave," Pharaoh told Moses. "Get out. Take your livestock. Take everything you own. Just go."

The Hebrews walked out of Egypt with all their possessions, their livestock, and even gold and silver given to them by the Egyptians as they went. Pharaoh had let God's people go.

As they walked out of Egypt, they were led by a pillar of fire by night and a pillar of cloud by day.

But they were not free yet.

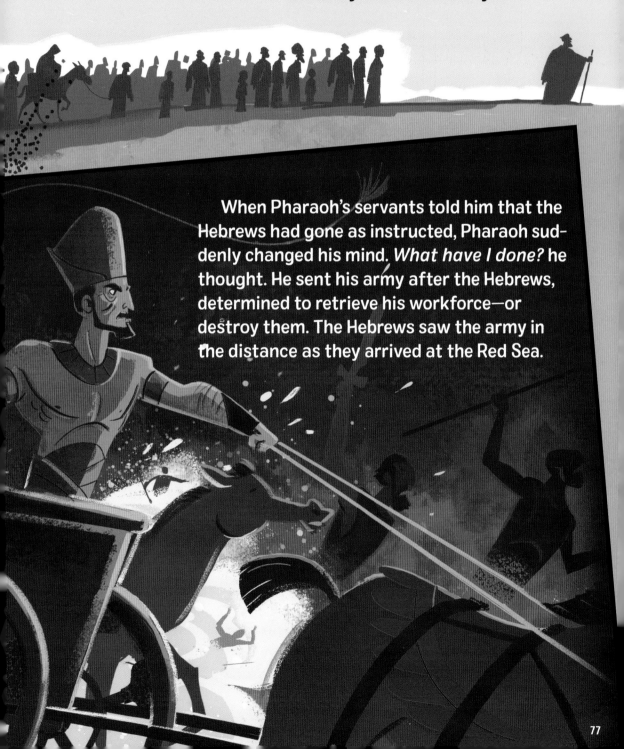

When Pharaoh's servants told him that the Hebrews had gone as instructed, Pharaoh suddenly changed his mind. *What have I done?* he thought. He sent his army after the Hebrews, determined to retrieve his workforce—or destroy them. The Hebrews saw the army in the distance as they arrived at the Red Sea.

"What will we do?" they cried. "Have we come here just to die?"

But God said to Moses, "Lift your hand toward the sea."

He did—and the sea parted! The water stood as though it had walls, and the people began to walk through on the dry ground as quickly as they could.

As the Egyptians began to cross the sea and the last of the Hebrews reached the other side, God brought the water crashing back together, destroying Pharaoh's army. No longer in danger, the Hebrews continued their journey.

But they were not free yet.

When God provided food in the wilderness, making it fall from the sky each morning, the people complained, longing for meat.

While God was giving them the Law—the rules of worship and life that defined them as His people—they made a golden calf and worshiped it.

When they reached the promised land, they feared the people who already lived there and believed their children would be killed, and they refused to enter.

On and on their disobedience went, because despite no longer being slaves in Egypt, they were not free yet. They were still slaves to their sin.

God showed them mercy as Moses interceded for them. When they grumbled about having no water, Moses struck a rock and water poured out. When they worshiped idols,

Moses pleaded for their lives before God, to prevent them from being wiped from the face of the earth. When they refused to enter the promised land, God promised that their children would conquer the land, but the adults who refused to enter would die in the wilderness.

The Israelites spent the next forty years wandering in the wilderness, waiting for the time when they could enter the promised land. But over time, they became bitter and complained against God and Moses.

"There is no food here, and the water is bitter," they complained, ignoring the food God provided each day and forgetting how God provided water from even impossible sources like rocks. God's provision wasn't enough for them.

God sent poisonous snakes throughout the camp, and many people died from snake bites. They realized they had sinned and begged Moses to intercede with God for them.

"Make a snake image and mount it on a pole," God said. "When anyone who is bitten looks at it, he will recover." Moses did what God commanded, and anyone who had been bitten was healed when they looked upon the bronze serpent.

Moses was Israel's mediator and their deliverer. He was their prophet and leader. But he couldn't solve their sin problem because he was a sinner too. At the end of his life, he addressed the people one final time and promised that another would come. Another Deliverer, another Mediator, another Prophet like him who was *greater* than him—Jesus.

Jesus was the One who could give them what they truly needed. The One who could provide them with bread from heaven. Who could give them living water. Who would set their captive hearts free. He was the One they needed, the way, **the truth**, and the life.

And just as the people were healed when they looked upon the bronze serpent, all who would look upon Jesus in faith would live.

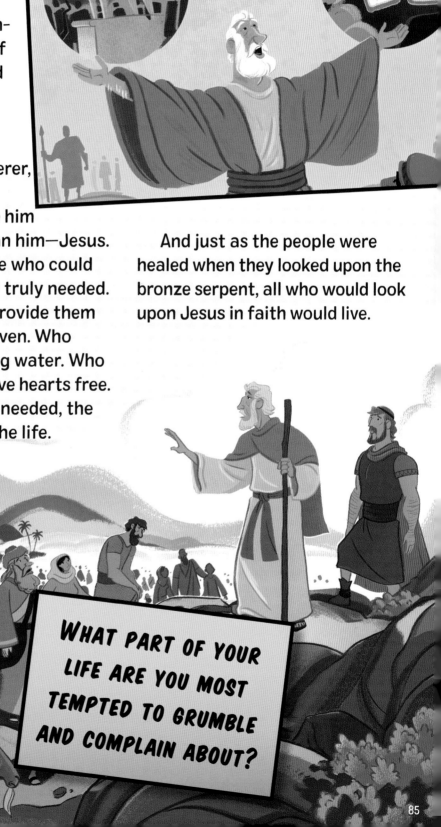

WHAT PART OF YOUR LIFE ARE YOU MOST TEMPTED TO GRUMBLE AND COMPLAIN ABOUT?

GOD GIVES HIS PEOPLE A HOME

Moses was dead. God's people had lost their leader, their mediator. The one who delivered the Law to them and spoke with God face-to-face, who had pleaded with God on their behalf so many times in the wilderness, was gone.

But Joshua was ready to take his place. Joshua, whose name means "the Lord saves," had served as Moses's assistant during their years wandering the wilderness outside the promised land. He was the one who would lead these children of former slaves to take hold of the land God promised them.

They crossed the Jordan river on dry ground, the waters parting before the presence of God as they had when Moses stretched out his hand before the Red Sea some forty years before.

But on the other side of the Jordan was their first challenge: Jericho.

The heavily fortified city was an intimidating sight to behold. Some saw it and were tempted to run. But Joshua sent two spies to explore the city, and what they learned astonished them.

They entered the house of a woman named Rahab, who hid them when the king learned of their presence and closed the gates.

I know that the Lord has given you this land. Everyone who lives here is panicking because of you!

When it was safe for them to go, Rahab made them promise to spare her family. The spies swore they would protect them all, risking their own lives for all who were found in this home. They returned to the camp and told Joshua what they saw in Jericho and heard from Rahab.

God said to Joshua, "I have handed Jericho over to you." It was time to conquer the city.

God gave them specific instructions for how to defeat Jericho. Although they were not normal combat instructions, the Israelites followed God's orders. For six days, they marched once around the city, and each time they blew seven trumpets. Then on the seventh day, they marched again. And then again. And again still. Seven times they marched around the perimeter of the city. Then they blew their horns, the soldiers shouted, and the walls of Jericho collapsed. What remained of Jericho's army was defeated, and by day's end, Israel was victorious. Rahab and her family joined them. The once mighty city of Jericho was a pile of burning rubble.

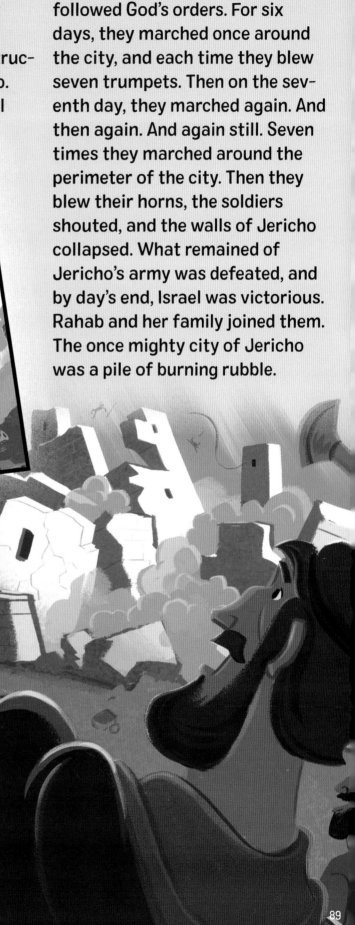

As God gave Israel victory over more cities and kingdoms, fear filled the land. With each victory in every region, on the east and west of the Jordan River, that fear spread. Everyone feared them. Every enemy fell. God even made the sun stand still to allow them victory! God gave them victory over every enemy until only a handful remained.

Through the conquest of the promised land, Joshua led courageously, but his time was nearing an end.

He gathered the people one final time, a people who struggled to remain faithful even as God worked in their midst.

Joshua reminded them of all the Lord had done for them—how He had rescued them from Egypt and brought them to the land He had promised to them, the land "flowing with milk and honey."

Get rid of your idols and worship Him only. But if it doesn't please you to worship the Lord, choose for yourselves:

Will you worship the gods our ancestors did, the gods of the people of this land, or the Lord?

As for me and my family, we will worship the Lord.

"Fear the Lord," he told them, "and worship Him in sincerity and truth."

The people swore they would worship the Lord and no other god. After all, He had done everything He said He would do. They had seen His faithfulness over and over again as they fought to conquer the promised land. But theirs was an empty promise.

These former slaves were free in body but were still slaves in spirit. They were trapped by their greatest love—a love of sin. And to overcome that, they would need Someone greater than Joshua, another whose name would remind the people that the Lord saves. One who would come not only from their own people, but from the family of Rahab, who joined them after their victory at Jericho.

Jesus, the One who would be their salvation.

IT'S EASY TO FORGET THAT GOD IS ALWAYS FAITHFUL TO US. HOW CAN WE REMEMBER THE WAYS GOD HAS BEEN FAITHFUL?

FAITHLESS PEOPLE AND A FAITHFUL GOD

After Joshua died there came a generation that did not remember all the Lord had done for them. They did evil in His sight, worshiping the false gods of the surrounding nations. So God sent others to rule over them in judgment of their sin. The people cried out to God for help, and God sent judges—men and women—to rescue them from their oppressors and lead them back to faithfulness. Some were faithful to the Lord and led the people faithfully.

Others were used by God to rescue the people even though they sinned against God continually.

When the Israelites sinned against the Lord by worshiping false gods, God allowed King Jabin of Canaan to cruelly oppress them for twenty years with the help of Sisera, the commander of Canaan's army.

They cried out for help, and God answered through Deborah, a prophetess from Ephraim whom God made judge over Israel.

Hasn't God commanded you to take ten thousand men into battle against Sisera? God will hand him over to you.

I will only go if you come with me.

I will come, but someone else will have the honor of the victory since you are afraid.

DEBORAH AND BARAK

95

Deborah sent for Barak, the leader of Israel's army.

When they came upon Sisera's army, Barak's troops fought fiercely, and the Lord threw Sisera and his forces into a panic.

Sisera ran from the battle and went to the tent of Jael, whose husband was Sisera's ally. Jael encouraged him to rest, gave him milk to drink and lulled him to sleep. Then she quietly crept over to the sleeping general and killed Sisera with a tent peg and a mallet.

Barak arrived and found Sisera dead. God's Word had been fulfilled. The victory belonged to Jael, not Barak. Barak and Deborah rejoiced and gave thanks to God, and Israel enjoyed forty years of peace.

But the people once again turned from the Lord, and were once again oppressed, this time by the Midianites. The angel of the Lord appeared to a man named Gideon.

THE LORD IS WITH YOU, VALIANT WARRIOR. GO AND DELIVER ISRAEL FROM THE GRIP OF MIDIAN.

Who am I to do this? My family is the weakest in Manasseh, and I am the youngest of my family.

I WILL BE WITH YOU.

GIDEON

After asking the Lord for a sign (twice), Gideon went to face the Midianites with thirty-two thousand troops, but God said this was too many. The Lord decreased his numbers, first to ten thousand and then to three hundred. With such a small army, victory could only come from the hand of God—which is exactly what God intended.

When Gideon spied on the Midianite camp, he discovered something unexpected: they were in fear. Of *him*. He returned to his army and split them up into three groups, giving each man a trumpet and an empty pitcher with a torch inside.

FOR THE LORD AND FOR GIDEON!

CRASH!

The sound of the shouting and trumpets threw the Midianites into confusion. They began furiously attacking one another, and when they regained their senses, most of the army was already dead. Gideon and his army pursued them.

Victorious, the Israelites sought to make Gideon their king. He refused, but he made an ephod—possibly a garment like the one the high priest of Israel wore or some kind of statue—and put it in his hometown. But it became a trap to him, his family, and all Israel as they worshiped it instead of God.

As time passed, the cycle of judgment and repentance continued. The nation would turn from God only to experience the consequences of their sin; then they would seek Him, but their devotion was, at best, half-hearted, much like that of Samson, perhaps the most famous of all the judges.

A Nazarite—a person consecrated to God's service—from birth, Samson was under a vow not to drink alcohol, to keep his hair uncut, and to avoid dead things. He was powerful, strong enough to kill a lion with his bare hands. He could have been a powerful leader, but he was more concerned with his own interests than the Lord's. Even so, God used this wayward judge to fulfill His purposes for His people.

Samson was in love with a woman, Delilah, who was a spy for the Philistines. The Philistines wanted to know the secret of Samson's great strength, so she asked him repeatedly what his secret was. First, Samson told her that tying him up with seven fresh bowstrings would remove his strength. She tried this, and it failed. Then he told her that new ropes would remove his strength, but that was also a lie. Finally, he told her the truth: if his hair was cut, he would lose his strength and be like other men. As Samson slept, Delilah cut his hair, and his strength left him.

"Samson! The Philistines are here!"

SAMSON

101

The Philistines attacked him, blinding him, and carried him away to Gaza where they made him grind grain in prison. Later, the Philistines gathered in the temple of their god, Dagon, to celebrate the capture of Samson. They called for Samson to entertain them. Humiliated, Samson stood between two pillars in the temple and prayed to the Lord.

STRENGTHEN ME, GOD, JUST ONCE MORE.

Strength filled his body. He began to push on the pillars. The building toppled and crushed everyone— including Samson himself, but in death, he defeated more Philistines than he had in life.

But Israel's troubles remained. Despite experiencing the consequences of their sin, they still worshiped false gods. They still rejected God. But someday, God would send another to judge His people, One who would only judge with right judgment, and lead His people away from sin forevermore.

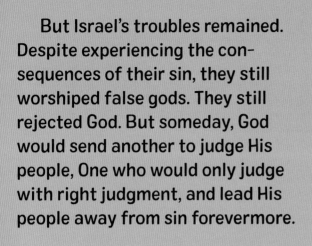

WHENEVER WE SIN, WE EXPERIENCE CONSEQUENCES. HOW HAVE THOSE CONSEQUENCES CHANGED YOUR BEHAVIOR?

A FAITHFUL REDEEMER

Naomi and Ruth arrived in Bethlehem, weary from their journey from Moab. Ten years earlier, Naomi, her husband, and their sons had traveled to Moab to escape a famine in Israel. Her husband and sons died there. She was left with two daughters-in-law who needed protection and care. She tried to send them back to their own people. One left, but the other, Ruth, refused to go.

"Where you go, I will go," Ruth told her. "Your people will be my people. Your God will be my God."

They traveled to Bethlehem, and Naomi was very bitter toward the Lord. When they arrived, it was time for the barley harvest. Ruth went to gather grain in a field that was owned by Boaz. When Boaz arrived at the fields, he asked one of his servants about Ruth.

His servant told him Ruth's story. Boaz went to her and told her to work only in his fields and stay close to the women working there.

He even asked her to sit and eat with him.

Ruth was confused but thankful. "Why are you being so kind?" she asked. He told Ruth he'd heard of her dedication to Naomi, how she had left behind everything she had ever known to remain with Naomi, including her family, friends, and even the gods she worshiped. Boaz prayed the Lord would bless Ruth because of her faithfulness.

Who is she?

At the end of the day, Ruth returned to Naomi with the barley she had harvested and the remaining grain from her meal. Ruth explained what had happened as Naomi ate.

"I worked in the field of a man named Boaz," she said. "He told me to stay and work in his fields until the harvest is complete."

"May the Lord bless him because of his kindness," Naomi said with joy. In her bitterness, she could only see what she had lost.

But hearing Boaz's name began to change that. After all, he was known for his kindness. He was a good, faithful, and well-respected man, and as a close relative of her husband, he was responsible to protect and keep them from harm in their time of need. For the first time in far too long, she began to feel her bitterness weaken. She began to hope.

Ruth continued to work in Boaz's fields, following just behind the other women. When the harvest was complete, Naomi told Ruth to think about her future.

She encouraged Ruth to go and speak with Boaz. Ruth agreed and after she got dressed in her best clothes, she went to speak with him. She found him asleep, and so she lay down at his feet. Around midnight he awoke and was startled to see a woman there!

"Who are you?" he asked.

"Ruth, your servant," she replied. "You're a close relative of Naomi's husband—will you keep us from harm?"

Boaz was pleased to see Ruth and agreed to help them by marrying her. But there was one problem— there was another man who was more closely related to them than he was. If the other man wanted to marry Ruth, he had priority over Boaz. But if he didn't, Boaz would.

Boaz sent Ruth home with a large amount of barley, as a sign of his commitment to helping her, and encouraged her to go home and wait for news. When morning came, Boaz went to the town gate, where the men conducted business, and met with the other relative. He shared Naomi and Ruth's situation.

"Will you marry Ruth and act as their redeemer?" he asked.

"I will not," he replied. "But you can."

Immediately Boaz went to Ruth and told her the news. They were married soon after, and about a year later she gave birth to a son whom they named Obed.

Obed grew up and had a son of his own, Jesse. And Jesse was the father of young man named David, who would become the great king of Israel, the king all other kings would be compared to. And from his family would come another Redeemer, one greater than His ancestor Boaz—a Redeemer who would give His life to rescue His bride, the Church, and destroy the power of sin forever.

GOD SENT HIS SON, JESUS, TO ACT AS A REDEEMER—A RESCUER AND PROTECTOR—FOR ALL WHO ASK HIM TO SAVE THEM FROM SIN. HOW HAVE YOU RESPONDED TO GOD'S OFFER OF RESCUE?

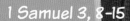

1 Samuel 3, 8–15

A KING AFTER THE PEOPLE'S HEART

Samuel heard a voice call out to him: "Samuel, Samuel!"

It was not the first time he heard the voice. Three times before, Samuel heard the voice call his name. Each time he thought it was Eli, the high priest of Israel, calling him. Eli eventually realized it had to be God speaking to him.

Samuel's mother, Hannah, desperate to have a child, vowed that if she did, her child would be dedicated to the Lord's service. When Samuel was born, she brought him to Eli so Samuel could be raised in God's house.

"If you hear the voice again," Eli told the boy, "say 'Speak, for your servant is listening.'"

Samuel returned to bed and heard the voice again.

SAMUEL, SAMUEL!

Speak, for your servant is listening.

God gave him a message—a warning of judgment to the high priest's family. Eli's sons were evil men who didn't love the Lord or respect their responsibilities as priests. God told Samuel that He was going to punish them for everything they had done. When Samuel told Eli what God said, Eli responded, "He is the Lord. Let Him do what He thinks is good."

As Samuel grew, the Lord was with him. Samuel was the final judge of Israel and was a prophet and a priest. But when he was an old man, the people grew restless and demanded a king to judge them, one like the kings of the other nations.

Samuel knew this was a terrible request. After all, *God* was their King. And a human king . . . well, he could take their property, their harvest, and even their children. But God said, "Give them what they want; they're not rejecting you, they're rejecting Me. But warn them and tell them of the rights a king will have over them."

And so Samuel warned them of all the rights a king would have over them, but they did not listen. They did not care. They insisted on having a king. So Samuel went to find one.

"I will send you a man from the land of Benjamin," God said. "Anoint him ruler over My people, Israel."

Saul was the son of a man named Kish from the tribe of Benjamin. He was more impressive than any other Israelite, standing a head taller than all the others. He looked like you would think a king should. When Samuel met him, Saul was searching for his lost donkeys.

THIS IS THE MAN I TOLD YOU ABOUT; HE WILL GOVERN MY PEOPLE.

Samuel poured oil over Saul's head and told him that the Lord had anointed him as ruler of His people. Samuel then sent Saul to Gibeah where he met a group of prophets. God's Spirit came upon Saul and began to prophesy as well.

Later, Samuel summoned the people to the town of Mizpah, where the people would gather to make important decisions for the nation. This time, they gathered to reveal the king. Samuel wanted to show that the choice of the king was God's, but Saul didn't come forward. *Where is he?* the people wondered.

"Has he come yet?" they asked. Then the people saw Saul, hiding among the supplies, afraid of the responsibility he had been given. They pulled him from his hiding place and were amazed at how he looked just as they thought a king should.

"Long live the king!" the people shouted. Samuel told them of the king's rights over them and then sent them back to their homes. Some of the people were happy and sent gifts to Saul, but others grumbled and wondered how this man could save them from their enemies.

Then the Ammonites attacked one of Israel's cities and called for their surrender. When the news of the attack reached Saul, he was furious and gathered an army of 330,000 men. His soldiers attacked the Ammonites and destroyed them. All of Israel rejoiced and praised God for their king. But their joy would not last.

Saul led the people into battle and to many victories. He rescued Israel from those who plundered them. But Saul was foolish; because he feared the people, he failed to obey the Lord's instructions. He made an offering on his own instead of waiting for Samuel. Later he made a rash oath that nearly resulted in the death of his son, Jonathan. Finally, he failed to obey the Lord again by leaving livestock and the king of the Amalekites alive instead of killing them as God instructed.

"What have you done?" Samuel asked, when he came to meet Saul and heard the noise of livestock. He already knew the answer. Saul had failed to listen to the Lord's instructions once again. He knew Saul would fail. It didn't surprise the old man, but it still grieved him.

Saul begged for forgiveness, but it was too late. His failure cost him the kingdom. God would not allow his rule to continue; another would take his place. After all, Saul was a king after the people's heart, exactly the king they asked for—like the kings of the other nations.

The Lord has removed the kingdom from you, and given it to another.

He looked the part, but he lacked character that made him worthy to rule. His years leading the nation were a reminder of the kind of king the people needed, the king the Lord had in mind. God would give them a king after God's own heart.

He would be a king from another tribe, the tribe of Judah. This king would love the Lord with all his heart, defeat the enemies of the nation, and rule faithfully. And from that king's family would come another King, a better King—Jesus, the King of kings, who never fails His people and rules from His throne forever.

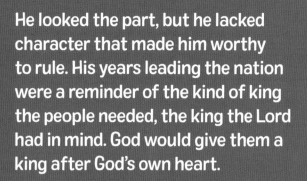

HOW DOES FOLLOWING JESUS PROTECT US FROM BEING PEOPLE PLEASERS?

A KING AFTER GOD'S HEART

*T*he giant laughed. Who was this boy coming out to face him? He wore no armor—and didn't even have a sword! Was this really the best warrior the Israelites had to offer?

The boy, David, was the youngest son of Jesse, son of Obed. He was a shepherd who had defeated bears and lions. He was a musician whose playing soothed King Saul when he was troubled by an evil spirit. And he was the one God had handed over the kingdom to, the one Samuel had anointed as king over all Israel.

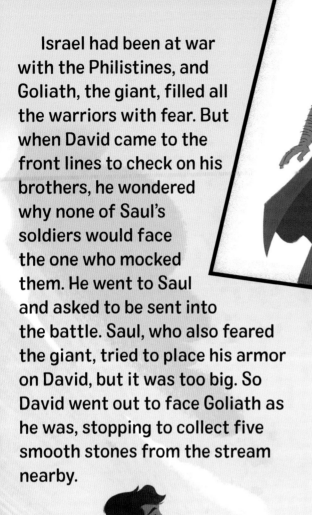

Israel had been at war with the Philistines, and Goliath, the giant, filled all the warriors with fear. But when David came to the front lines to check on his brothers, he wondered why none of Saul's soldiers would face the one who mocked them. He went to Saul and asked to be sent into the battle. Saul, who also feared the giant, tried to place his armor on David, but it was too big. So David went out to face Goliath as he was, stopping to collect five smooth stones from the stream nearby.

You come against me with a sword, spear, and javelin, but I come against you in the name of the Lord of Armies, the God of the ranks of Israel—you have defied Him.

Today, the Lord will hand you over to me. Today, I'll strike you down, remove your head, and give the corpses of the Philistine camp to the birds of the sky and the wild creatures of the earth.

Then all the world will know that Israel has a God, and this whole assembly will know that it is not by sword or by spear that the Lord saves, for the battle is the Lord's. He will hand you over to us.

David rushed toward Goliath. He reached his hand into his bag, took a stone, dropped it in his sling, and flung it toward the giant.

The stone struck him in the forehead, and Goliath
fell to the ground, dead. The Israelites were filled
with hope, and they rushed into battle against the
remaining Philistines, who began to flee when their
champion fell.

After this the Lord continued to grow David's reputation as a warrior, and he soon became the most admired man in Israel—even more than Saul himself. Saul became jealous of David because he could see that the Lord was with David. Saul even attempted to kill David by pinning him to the wall with a spear, but David escaped. Then Saul offered his daughter, Michal, as a bride if David would be a warrior for Saul and fight the Lord's battles. Perhaps then, Saul thought, David would be killed by the Philistines. But the Lord continued to give David victory.

Madness overcame Saul. He was determined to kill David, his son-in-law and rival. After another failed attempt on his life, David fled. He spent years as a fugitive, always evading Saul and his men. David even spared Saul's life in a cave once, refusing to raise a hand against God's anointed.

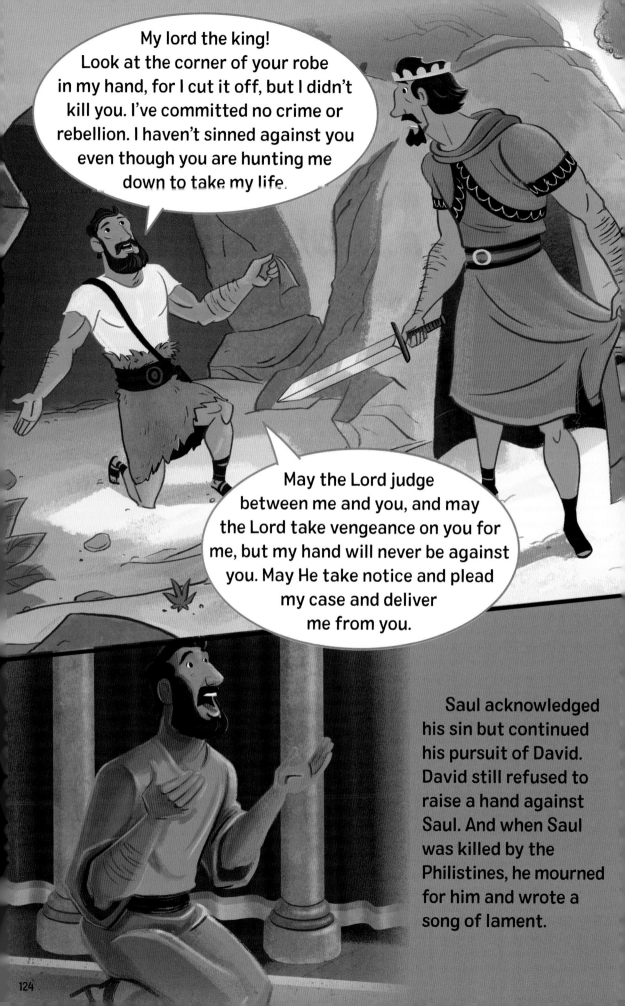

My lord the king! Look at the corner of your robe in my hand, for I cut it off, but I didn't kill you. I've committed no crime or rebellion. I haven't sinned against you even though you are hunting me down to take my life.

May the Lord judge between me and you, and may the Lord take vengeance on you for me, but my hand will never be against you. May He take notice and plead my case and deliver me from you.

Saul acknowledged his sin but continued his pursuit of David. David still refused to raise a hand against Saul. And when Saul was killed by the Philistines, he mourned for him and wrote a song of lament.

When David took his throne, he returned the ark of the covenant to Shiloh, where the tent of meeting was established. He danced in the streets in front of it, worshiping the Lord (even as his wife, Saul's daughter Michal, thought he was shaming himself). And when the war between Saul's family and his was over, he showed God's kindness to those who remained, bringing Mephibosheth, Jonathan's son, into his home and letting him eat at his table.

For forty years, David ruled over Israel as a faithful king. And God made a promise to him that he would have a descendent who would be a greater King than he was. He would rule from an eternal throne, and of His kingdom there would be no end. He would be the King of kings and Lord of lords. That King was Jesus, who would defeat a greater foe than David's giant and lead His people into victory, who would show God's kindness to all by giving up His life to pay for the sins of all who believe.

HOW CAN YOU DEMONSTRATE GOD'S KINDNESS TO SOMEONE YOU KNOW TODAY?

A KING WHO NEEDED A NEW HEART

David listened intently as Nathan told him of two men, one rich and the other poor. The rich man had very large flocks, but the poor man had only one small lamb. He raised this lamb, and she grew up with his children; he loved her as though she were his daughter.

A traveler stayed with the rich man, but the rich man wouldn't take one of his own sheep to feed his guest. So he took the poor man's only lamb.

King David was furious. "Who is this man? He deserves to die for what he has done!"

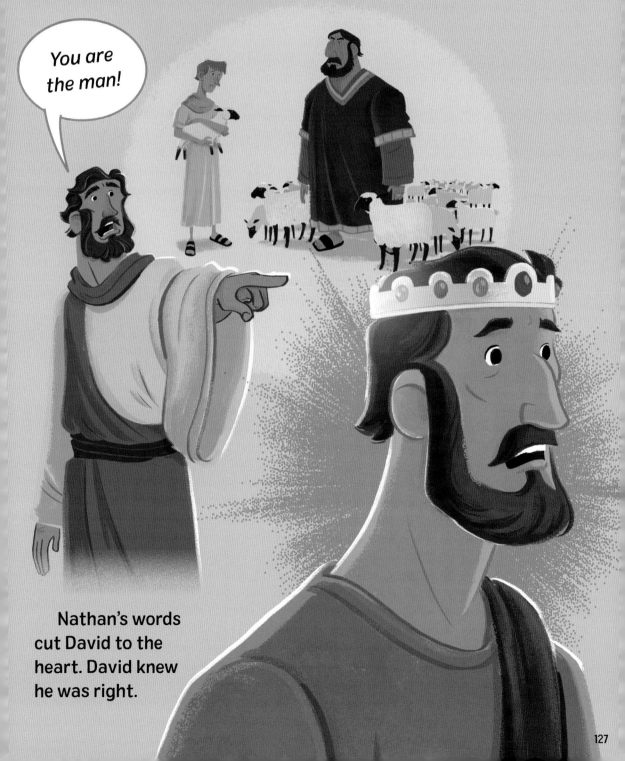

You are the man!

Nathan's words cut David to the heart. David knew he was right.

Months earlier, when Israel was at war with its enemies, King David had remained behind in Jerusalem. He'd gone out onto the balcony to enjoy the night air and had seen Bathsheba out on the rooftop of her home taking a bath. He should have looked away, but his eyes were fixed.

"Who is that?" He had asked.

"Uriah's wife," his servant answered.

"Bring her to see me," David ordered.

And David sinned against Uriah and the Lord.

Later, Bathsheba came to David and told him she was expecting a baby. So David tried to cover up his sin. He called Uriah home from the front lines and encouraged him to indulge in all the comforts of home. But Uriah slept on the stoop in front of David's home.

Since his plan didn't work, David wrote a message for Uriah to deliver to Joab, the commander of the army: "Put Uriah at the front of the fiercest fighting, then withdraw from him so that he is struck down and dies."

Joab did as he was instructed, and Uriah was killed.

David took Bathsheba as his wife, and they welcomed a baby boy into their family. David had thought his sin was covered up. But nothing could be hidden from God.

David admitted to Nathan, "I have sinned against the Lord."

David knew that even when no one else was looking, God could see all. All his sin was on display. And so he asked God to cleanse him of his

sin, to wash him clean and give him a new heart—a heart free from the sin that had led to the death of Uriah.

God forgave his sin, but there would still be consequences. His family would never be at peace. David's children would commit horrible crimes against one another, his son would try to overthrow him, and Bathsheba's child would die.

But the throne would not be taken from David. The promise God had made to establish David's kingdom forever stood firm. A King would come from his family, One who would sit on the throne forever. A King who would wash away the sin that stained David's heart, and, by faith, make it new. And centuries later, that King was revealed: Jesus, the One who restores the joy of salvation to all who come to Him with humble and contrite spirits.

I have sinned against the Lord!

WHY DOES IT MATTER THAT ALL SIN IS AGAINST GOD? HOW DOES IT CHANGE HOW WE RESPOND TO SIN IN OUR LIVES?

A KING BETRAYED BY HIS WANDERING HEART

Even the wisest man to ever live wasn't wise enough to escape his own sin.

Solomon was the youngest son of King David, and he was chosen to be the next king of Israel. Solomon was not the one most people would have expected to be the next king. He was young and inexperienced. Most people would have expected Adonijah, Solomon's elder brother, to be the next king (Adonijah certainly thought so). But Solomon was the one God wanted on the throne. After Solomon became king, the Lord appeared to him in a dream.

ASK. WHAT SHOULD I GIVE YOU?

Give Your servant wisdom so I can judge Your people and discern between good and evil.

I WILL GIVE YOU A WISE AND DISCERNING HEART, AND I WILL ALSO GIVE YOU WHAT YOU DID NOT ASK FOR: BOTH RICHES AND HONOR, SO THAT NO KING WILL BE YOUR EQUAL DURING YOUR ENTIRE LIFE.

The beginning of Solomon's reign was full of promise. He led the kingdom wisely and his decrees were just. He wrote thousands of proverbs and songs, some of which we can still read today in the books of Proverbs and Psalms. He expanded the nation to its largest size and richest economy, and his reputation was known throughout all the world.

And most importantly, he built the temple in Jerusalem, the place where God would dwell among His people. The place where all Israel would go to worship their God. But it wasn't just for Israel. Solomon prayed it would be a place where people from *every* nation would meet with God and worship Him.

Solomon reigned in a time
of great peace and prosperity.
It was as close to heaven on
earth as you could imagine.
Until it wasn't.

Despite all his great wisdom, Solomon suffered from a wandering heart. He collected a great fortune for himself. He married many women who did not worship the Lord and had 12,000 horsemen and 1,400 chariots. He even built himself a palace greater than the temple itself. And all these things turned his heart from the God who had given him all things. Claiming to be wise, he became a fool.

Solomon's foolishness led to disaster. He began to treat his workforces harshly, making demands that were too difficult for the workers. He started worshiping the gods of his wives. His folly led to the fall of the next generation, as his son Rehoboam's arrogance led to the kingdom being split in two.

And it became worse still. The Northern Kingdom of Israel immediately fell into idolatry, worshiping two golden calves. And every king that followed fell further and further into sin, rejecting God at every turn. Finally, the kingdom was destroyed by foreign invaders.

Even though God's people had disobeyed Him, God was still good. Despite Solomon's unfaithfulness, God was faithful. He preserved a kingdom for David's family—the Southern Kingdom of Judah. Judah was the tribe God promised would lead Israel centuries before when Jacob blessed his sons. It was the tribe Solomon's family came from. From Solomon's family came other kings, some of whom led God's people into sin, while others led the people to turn from sin.

And eventually from this family came another King, whom Solomon at his best points forward to, and at his worst reminds us of our need for. The King who is not simply wise, but *is* wisdom. The King who is gentle and whose commands are not too much for His people. The King who never leads His people into temptation, but gave up His life so all who believe will be with Him for all eternity.

HOW CAN GOD'S WISDOM DRAW US CLOSER TO HIM?

1 Kings 18; 2 Kings 2–10, 13

THE POWER OF GOD AND THE JUDGMENT OF GOD

I am the only remaining prophet of the Lord, but Baal's prophets are 450 men. Let two bulls be given to us. They will prepare one for a sacrifice, and I will prepare the other. Neither of us will light the fire. Instead, you will call on the name of your god, and I will call on the name of the Lord. The one who answers with fire is the true God.

The people had long ago abandoned the worship of God. Israel and her kings had chosen the gods of the nations. But God continued to send prophets to warn the people and plead with them to turn from their sin before it was too late.

Among the greatest of these was Elijah. He was powerful in word and deed, offering words of warning, speaking God's Word, and performing many signs and wonders—even raising a boy from the dead!

As Elijah watched the false prophets cry out to their god, asking Baal to send fire from heaven to consume their offering, he already knew what would happen: Nothing. Their god could not hear them. It could not speak. It had no power because it was nothing.

But his God—the true God—He was mighty, and He would demonstrate His power to His wayward people.

Fire fell from the sky and consumed the offering, the wood, and even the rocks that made up the altar. The people were amazed and fell down and declared that the Lord, the God of their ancestors, was the true God.

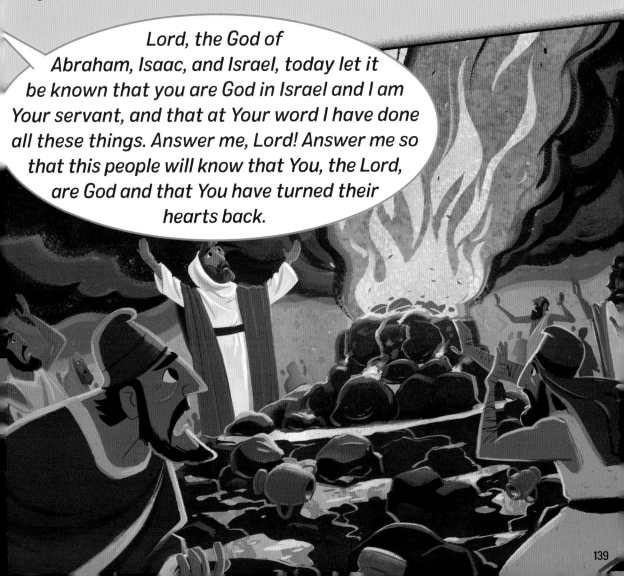

Lord, the God of Abraham, Isaac, and Israel, today let it be known that you are God in Israel and I am Your servant, and that at Your word I have done all these things. Answer me, Lord! Answer me so that this people will know that You, the Lord, are God and that You have turned their hearts back.

But their worship was temporary. Before the next day was through, Elijah was on the run from those who wished to kill him.

But even so, he was not alone. God was with him. God had protected a group of Israelites who were still faithful to Him. And God provided another prophet to continue Elijah's mission to call Israel to turn away from their sins when he was gone.

When it was time for Elijah to go and be with the Lord, Elisha, his assistant, followed him, first to Bethel and then to the Jordan River. When they reached the Jordan, Elisha made one request of Elijah.

They continued walking and talking for a while. Then a whirlwind appeared and a chariot came from the sky. Elijah was carried up in the chariot and taken to the Lord. And although he went to be with the Lord, he did not die.

Please, let me inherit two portions of your spirit.

Elisha saw everything. Once Elijah was gone, Elisha saw his master's cloak on the ground. He picked it up and left to continue Elijah's work.

I am healed!

Elisha would do even greater works than his master. He warned the descendants of Israel's evil king, Ahab, that God's judgment was coming. He poured oil over a man named Jehu, naming him the king of Israel and the one who would destroy Ahab's family. Elisha cleansed lepers. He fed more than a hundred people with twenty small loaves of bread. He raised a boy from the dead. And even after he died, God's power continued to show itself through Elisha; some Israelite men threw a dead man into his grave. When the man's body touched Elisha's bones, the body was revived and stood up!

Both prophets revealed the power of God to His people, and both pointed to another Prophet who would do even mightier wonders than either Elijah or Elisha: He would feed thousands, heal the sick, cleanse lepers, proclaim good news to captives, and even raise the dead! Jesus was the One both Elijah and Elisha pointed to.

He was the One who would show the power of God by taking upon Himself the judgment for sin in order to rescue His people from their sins.

GOD SHOWED HIS POWER THROUGH THE PROPHETS ELIJAH AND ELISHA IN MANY WAYS. HOW DOES GOD SHOW HIS POWER THROUGH YOUR LIFE?

SALVATION BELONGS TO THE LORD

Who has brought this storm upon us?" the sailors cried. Waves crashed against the sides of the ship, water weighing it down. Surely they would sink, and all on board would die. But down in the lower decks, the prophet Jonah slept peacefully.

"Get up!" the men cried. They cast lots—a method of rolling dice or some other kind of marker to discern the will of God—to try to learn who was the cause of this terrible storm. It was Jonah.

"Who are you?" the sailors asked.

"I am a Hebrew and a worshiper of the Lord."

The men were terrified. "What have you done?"

God had called Jonah to deliver a warning to the people of Nineveh. But Jonah hated the Ninevites and wanted them to face God's judgment. So he had boarded a ship sailing toward Tarshish, a city in the other direction. But God wouldn't let him go that easily.

"Throw me overboard," Jonah told the sailors. "Then the sea will be calm for you."

They picked Jonah up and threw him into the sea, asking that God not hold his life against them.

When Jonah hit the surface of the water, the storm stopped. A great fish swallowed Jonah. Though the fish might otherwise have been his grave, after three days, God commanded it to spit Jonah up onto dry land.

"Now, go to Ninevah," God commanded him again. And Jonah did.

When he arrived, Jonah proclaimed, "In forty days Nineveh will be demolished!" Then he waited to see what would happen next. Jonah wanted to see this great city destroyed.

But that didn't happen. Instead the people believed God and turned from their sin. Even the king issued a decree commanding everyone to turn from their evil ways and believe in the Lord. God heard their prayers and did not destroy the city. Instead He turned His attention once again to His furious prophet.

This is what I knew would happen. It's why I went to Tarshish in the first place! I knew that You are a gracious and compassionate God, slow to anger, abounding in faithful love, and one who relents from sending disaster. I knew You wouldn't destroy them like I wanted.

IS IT RIGHT FOR YOU TO BE ANGRY? MAY I NOT CARE ABOUT THE GREAT CITY OF NINEVEH, WHICH HAS MORE THAN A HUNDRED AND TWENTY THOUSAND PEOPLE WHO CANNOT DISTINGUISH BETWEEN THEIR RIGHT AND THEIR LEFT?

Jonah gave no answer. He could not, because he already knew the answer. In the belly of the whale, he remembered that salvation belongs to the Lord. And God's desire was to save any who would turn from their sin and believe in Him. There were no lengths He would not go to accomplish this goal.

Centuries later, He would make this clear by sending another Prophet—One who wept over a city facing judgment—who would spend three days in His own grave and rise again. A Prophet who would proclaim the message Jonah knew to be true: salvation belongs to the Lord.

GOD WANTS US TO SHOW MERCY TO OTHERS, EVEN OUR ENEMIES. HOW CAN WE SHOW THIS MERCY TO OTHERS TODAY?

THE PROMISED RESCUER

After Solomon's reign and Israel split in two, the Lord sent prophets to both the Northern and Southern Kingdoms.

Some, like Hosea, were called to act as living lessons: through his marriage to and pursuit of the unfaithful Gomer, Hosea was showing the people God's pursuit of them.

HOSEA

Others, like Obadiah came with more direct promises of restoration and blessing.

OBADIAH

JOEL

Others still, like Joel, gave messages of powerful warnings of judgment and calls to repentance.

Many others came with special messages—messages that pointed forward to something greater. To Someone greater: the Messiah, the Rescuer of God's people.

Zechariah shared a vision of the high priest, Joshua, being accused by Satan as he stood in filthy robes before the angel of the Lord. But the angel called for his filthy clothes to be removed, symbolizing the removal of his sin.

ZECHARIAH

The prophet Jeremiah shared God's message about sin and the problem of the human heart. He proclaimed that God would give a new covenant to His people—a covenant that was different than the one He made with their ancestors. A covenant that would give them new hearts, not new commands. A covenant that would bring forgiveness and hope.

JEREMIAH

EZEKIEL

Ezekiel offered hope of restoration when God showed him a valley of dry bones. There was no life in them, but the Lord gave them life again. In the same way, God was going to give life to His people and place His Spirit in them so they would live.

153

But the most power-ful message was Isaiah's prophecy of the Messiah as the suffering servant. The servant would carry the burden of God's peo-ple's sins and would be crushed—killed—taking their punishment so they could have peace with God. It was a message of hope, of rescue as the servant gave His life for many:

ISAIAH

...HE HIMSELF BORE OUR SICKNESSES,
AND HE CARRIED OUR PAINS;
BUT WE IN TURN REGARDED HIM STRICKEN,
STRUCK DOWN BY GOD, AND AFFLICTED.

BUT HE WAS PIERCED BECAUSE OF OUR REBELLION,
CRUSHED BECAUSE OF OUR INIQUITIES;
PUNISHMENT FOR OUR PEACE WAS ON HIM,
AND WE ARE HEALED BY HIS WOUNDS.

WE ALL WENT ASTRAY LIKE SHEEP;
WE ALL HAVE TURNED TO OUR OWN WAY;
AND THE LORD HAS PUNISHED HIM
FOR THE INIQUITY OF US ALL. (ISAIAH 53:4-6)

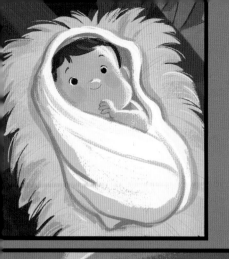

Every time the prophets spoke of the Messiah, it was with this sense of hope, of anticipation. And every message from the prophets built upon the others to give a picture of who this Messiah, this Rescuer really was: A descendant of David. A Nazarene born in Bethlehem. A servant, and a King, who was God Himself.

Jesus of Nazareth, the Messiah, the Son of God. The One who would remove the sins of all who believe, and cover them with His righteousness. The One who would give them new hearts by faith. The One who would place His Spirit within them and give them new life.

The One who was pierced for our rebellion, crushed because of our sins, and heals us by His wounds.

GOD'S MESSAGES ABOUT THE MESSIAH WERE MEANT TO GIVE HIS PEOPLE HOPE WHILE THEY WAITED FOR JESUS TO COME. HOW DOES WHAT YOU KNOW ABOUT JESUS GIVE YOU HOPE WHILE YOU WAIT FOR HIM TO RETURN?

THE KINGDOMS FALL

For more than 325 years, Israel and Judah had failed to obey the Lord. They ignored the warnings in the Law and the words of His prophets. God had been patient with them, but it was time for judgment to come.

From the beginning, the Northern Kingdom had abandoned the Lord. Its kings led the people into great sin, worshiping false gods and golden calves. For two hundred years their kings did evil in the sight of the Lord, and with rare exception, each was worse than the last.

Their final king, Hoshea, was on the throne for six years before the Assyrians attacked and surrounded Samaria. Three years later, Samaria was captured and Israel fell. The people were taken away and dispersed throughout the cities of the Medes, another nation under Assyrian rule. But even in captivity, Israel did not repent. They despised the Lord just as their ancestors did.

Judah, the Southern Kingdom, fared no better. After the kingdom had split, Judah's kings abandoned the Lord and followed the practices of the Northern Kingdom of Israel and of the nations. But the nation returned to the Lord for significant periods. Asa, Jotham, Jehoshaphat, Hezekiah, and Josiah all led the nation in these seasons of renewal. But it would not last. Evil kings, proud and foolish kings, would take the throne and lead the people back into sin. A hundred and fifteen years after Israel fell, Babylon surrounded Jerusalem. The temple was sacked and burned to the ground. The palace was destroyed. The walls were broken down. The city fell and its people were led away in chains, sent to live in Babylon.

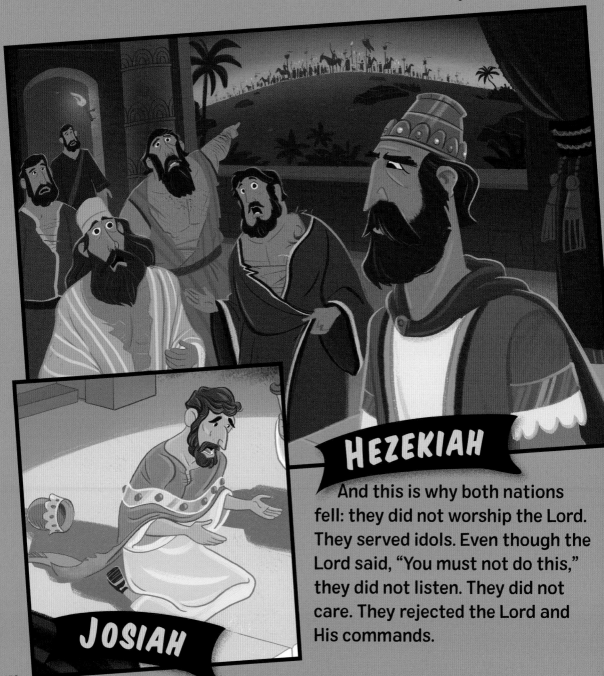

HEZEKIAH

JOSIAH

And this is why both nations fell: they did not worship the Lord. They served idols. Even though the Lord said, "You must not do this," they did not listen. They did not care. They rejected the Lord and His commands.

But although they rejected Him and He had sent them into captivity, God was not finished with His people. He sent them a message through the prophet Jeremiah, a promise:

Build houses and live in them. Plant gardens and eat their produce. Have children and grow your families. Multiply there; do not decrease. Pursue the well-being of the city I have sent you to. Pray to the Lord on the city's behalf, for when it thrives, you will thrive.

When seventy years in Babylon are complete, I will restore you. For I know the plans I have for you, plans for your well-being, not for disaster, to give you a future and a hope. You will call to Me and come and pray to Me, and I will listen to you. You will seek Me and find Me when you search for Me with all your heart. I will restore your fortunes and gather you from all the nations and places where I banished you. I will restore you to the place from which I sent you.

The people would remain in Babylon for seventy years, and God would use them for His purposes during that time. They would be restored when they turned back to God, just as He promised.

But this restoration wouldn't be the end of the story. It was only a step toward the promise God made in the beginning. A greater restoration was coming for people from every nation of the earth. This restoration would put an end to sin and death and see people enjoy a relationship with God forever and ever. It's the restoration of sinners who call upon the name of Jesus Christ, the Messiah.

SIN ALWAYS HAS CONSEQUENCES, BUT GOD PROMISES TO RESTORE ALL WHO CALL TO HIM. HOW HAVE YOU SEEN THIS IN YOUR OWN LIFE?

Daniel 3, 6

"EVEN IF HE DOESN'T..."

Despite having impressed their overseers—and even King Nebuchadnezzar himself when Daniel interpreted his dreams, Daniel, Shadrach, Meshach, and Abednego probably shouldn't have had the place of honor they enjoyed in Babylon. They were captives from the fallen kingdom Judah, taken as slaves.

They even refused to eat certain foods and insisted on worshiping their own God. Why couldn't they just go along with everyone else?

Many Babylonians began to look for opportunities to plot against them. One day Nebuchadnezzar built a golden statue and commanded that everyone worship it whenever they heard the sound of music. Those who failed to do so would be put to death in a fiery furnace. The Babylonians had their first opportunity when Shadrach, Meshach, and Abednego refused to bow.

Will you worship the statue? If you don't, you'll be executed.

Nebuchadnezzar, we don't need to answer your question. If the God we serve exists, then He can rescue us.

But even if He doesn't, we will not worship the gold statue.

Enraged, Nebuchadnezzar commanded they be thrown into the fire. But as he looked on, he was shocked—not only were the three alive, there was a fourth person inside with them, one who looked like "a son of the gods."

Nebuchadnezzar marveled and commanded they be released from the furnace immediately. Then he made a decree that anyone who said anything offensive about their God—the true God— would be put to death.

But this wouldn't be the last time their insistence on following God would cause conflict.

Years after Nebuchadnezzar's reign, Daniel served in the court of another king, Darius the Mede. He held a place of honor, and the other officials again desired to get rid of him. But they knew Daniel was a law-abiding man and he could only be charged with a crime if it concerned the law of his God. So they went to the king.

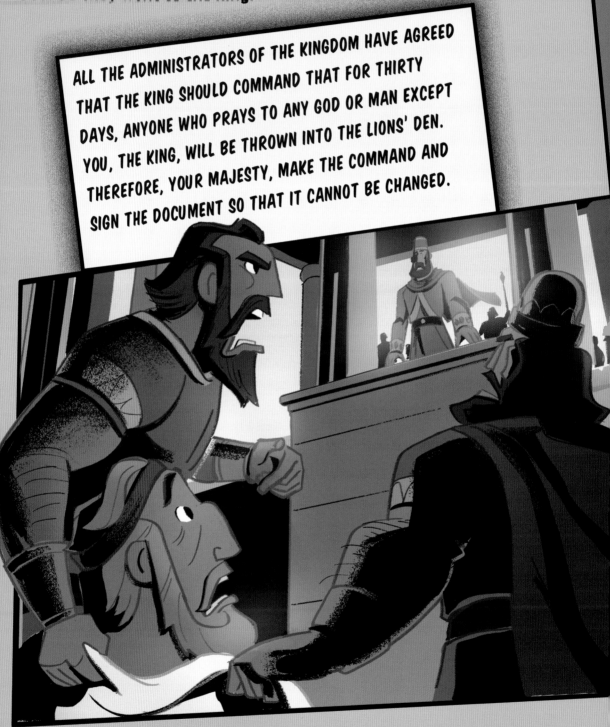

ALL THE ADMINISTRATORS OF THE KINGDOM HAVE AGREED THAT THE KING SHOULD COMMAND THAT FOR THIRTY DAYS, ANYONE WHO PRAYS TO ANY GOD OR MAN EXCEPT YOU, THE KING, WILL BE THROWN INTO THE LIONS' DEN. THEREFORE, YOUR MAJESTY, MAKE THE COMMAND AND SIGN THE DOCUMENT SO THAT IT CANNOT BE CHANGED.

Darius signed the command, and when Daniel heard about it, he did what he always did: he went into his house, opened the windows, and prayed, giving thanks to God.

The officials watching Daniel went to Darius and reported Daniel's violation of this new law. Darius was grieved, realizing he had been tricked, but he had to throw Daniel into the lion's den.

The den was sealed, and the king went to his palace. That night the king could not sleep; his concern for Daniel was too great. At the first light of dawn, he got up and raced to the den.

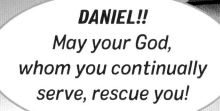

DANIEL!!
May your God,
whom you continually
serve, rescue you!

Overjoyed, Darius commanded Daniel be taken out of the den. Then he had the men who accused Daniel brought and thrown to the lions. They hadn't even reached the bottom before the lions had killed them.

These four men, Shadrach, Meshach, Abednego, and Daniel, refused to compromise what they believed. They faced death for the sake of faithfulness, and God blessed them and rescued them from danger. But even if He hadn't protected them, they still would have obeyed. They knew obeying their God was better than going along with everyone else.

My God sent his angel and shut the lions' mouths; and they haven't harmed me, for I was found innocent before God.

WHERE OR WHEN IS IT MOST DIFFICULT FOR YOU TO OBEY GOD?

And generations later, another faithful man would face this same dilemma—a challenge to worship a false god in order to gain the world. He would cast the tempter away, knowing that it did not profit anyone to gain the world but lose their soul.

He would also be sentenced to death, but He would not escape it. Instead, He would give His life willingly as payment for sin—and the entire world would be blessed through Him.

"FOR SUCH A TIME AS THIS"

Who knows, perhaps you have come to your royal position for such a time as this.

Mordecai's words echoed in Esther's ears as she approached the throne room. She was a Jew, a child of an exile from the land of Judah. Her uncle, Mordecai, had raised her as though she were his own daughter when her parents died.

She was also the queen.

Mordecai had instructed her to keep her heritage a secret. Now she was being asked to risk everything, all because of one man's hatred for her people. Haman was a very proud man and one of King Ahasuerus's honored officials. All the kings officials bowed down to him except Mordecai the Jew. So Haman devised a plan: he was going to wipe out all the Jewish people. Orders had already gone out to all corners of the kingdom. Preparations were being made. And Mordecai, the one Haman hated most, would be hanged on the gallows he was constructing.

Esther knew her position would not spare her from sharing the same fate as all the other Jews. But maybe Mordecai was right. Perhaps she *had* come to her royal position for such a time as this.

Esther knew she had to speak to the king, but she had not been summoned. Unless the king extended his scepter to welcome her, she would face the penalty of death for coming to him uninvited. She had asked all the Jews in the city to fast and pray for her. She and her servants did the same.

Esther was prepared to make her move. She had a plan, and if she perished she perished.

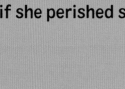

Esther entered the throne room and approached the king. Ahasuerus was pleased to see her and extended his scepter.

If it pleases the king, may the king and Haman come today to the banquet I have prepared for them.

The king and Haman did as Esther asked. At the banquet the king again asked Esther what he could do. She invited them both to another banquet the next night. Then she would tell him everything.

But that night the king struggled to sleep, so he requested the records of events be brought to him. He found a record of Mordecai having saved him from an assassination plot.

Nothing.

What's been done to honor this man?

Ahasuerus called for Haman, who was the only man still in the court.

What should be done for a man I wish to honor?

Haman was overjoyed. *Finally, I can tell him what he should do for me*, he thought, his pride radiating from every pore.

Have them bring a royal garment the king has worn and a horse the king has ridden with a royal crown on its head. Have one of the king's most noble officials clothe the man and parade him on the horse through the city square and proclaim, "This is what is done for the man the king wants to honor."

PERFECT! Go and do this at once for Mordecai the Jew.

Haman was devastated, his pride replaced with shame. *Mordecai?* He thought. *How could the king want to honor him?* Haman did as he was commanded and honored Mordecai, the man he planned to execute. He clothed Mordecai in the king's robe and paraded him through the town square as Haman had hoped would be done for him. Then he fled home, his shame too much to bear. Shortly after, the king's servants came to bring him to the banquet with Queen Esther.

During the banquet the king asked Esther what troubled her.

YAY MORDECAI!!

My people and I have been sold to destruction, death, and extermination.

Who has done this?

*This evil man—**HAMAN!***

The king was *furious* and searched for Haman.

Haman begged Queen Esther to save his life. The king returned and saw Haman. "Would he hurt the queen in my own palace?" he shouted.

The king executed Haman, hanging him on the very gallows that Haman had constructed for Mordecai's execution. Orders were issued to arm the Jews and allow them to defend themselves against any attackers so that they might be spared.

Victorious, the Jews celebrated. They had been spared because, although He hadn't said a word, God had placed Esther in her royal position for such a time as this. He had worked all things according to His purposes, to protect and bring honor to His people.

And centuries later He would do it again. At just the right time He would send another to rescue His people.

A Prince who would work all things for the good of His people.

A Prince who would give up His life.

A Prince who would pick it up again.

IF GOD IS WORKING OUT ALL THINGS FOR OUR GOOD, HOW DOES THAT CHANGE HOW WE LIVE?

THE RETURN TO THE PROMISED LAND

*I*t had been seventy years since God's people had been taken into captivity by the Babylonians. Seventy years since their sin had resulted in their punishment. In that time, they had been humbled, nearly eradicated, and blessed as God used them to seek the well-being of the city where they found themselves.

During that time, God also judged the Babylonians, using the Persians to bring their empire to an end. And in the first year of King Cyrus of Persia's rule, a decree was issued: any of the Hebrews who wished to return to their land were free to do so. Seven months later, the people gathered in Jerusalem and offered a sacrifice to the Lord for the first time since they had been carried off to Babylon.

REPENT!!

Then the difficult work began. First they began to rebuild the temple. When the foundation had been laid, many of the people rejoiced. But the oldest of the people, the ones who remembered the first temple, wept.

As the rebuilding continued, the Jews' enemies opposed the construction. They sent letters to the king of Persia, demanding he stop their work. They bribed the king's officials. They harassed the Jews and made them afraid to keep building. Finally the king commanded them to stop all their construction. For more than ten years the temple remained unfinished until the second year of king Darius's reign. At that time God sent prophets to the people, who were focused on rebuilding their own homes instead of building the temple. The people repented, and construction began once again.

Opposition resumed, but the Jews sent a letter to Darius and requested he search the archives for Cyrus's command that the temple be rebuilt. When it was discovered, the opposition ceased. Four years later the temple was completed. That same year God's people celebrated the Passover—the feast remembering their rescue from Egypt—for the first time in more than seventy years.

Many years passed. The temple was complete, but the city of Jerusalem remained in ruins. Nehemiah, the cupbearer of King Artaxerxes, was heartbroken when he heard about the state of the city. When he stood before the king, his sadness was obvious to everyone, including the king.

"Why are you sad?" the king asked. Nehemiah prayed and told the king. Artaxerxes commanded that Nehemiah be allowed to go to Jerusalem and rebuild its walls. The king wrote letters for safe passage, released Nehemiah from his service as cupbearer, and commanded that he be given supplies to complete his task.

NEHEMIAH

Several months later, Nehemiah arrived in Jerusalem and began the work of rebuilding the walls. He met opposition from neighboring nations—the Ammonites, Arabs and Ashdodites—and there was even a plan to kill Nehemiah. But Nehemiah persevered, commanding the people to work with a sword in one hand and a trowel in the other. And after fifty-two days the walls were completed.

EZRA

But construction wasn't the only problem Jews faced. Ezra the priest arrived in Jerusalem during this time and found the people had forgotten the Law. They were marrying with the people of the surrounding nations and beginning to commit all the sins that had sent them into exile in the first place! Ezra taught the Law to the people and led them to repentance. And God continued to send prophets to lead the people to faithfulness.

Despite all their challenges, Ezra, Nehemiah, and other faithful leaders persevered. They rebuilt the city. Worship resumed, and for a time, the people were at peace.

But they were not free. They could not rule themselves as they saw fit. They were still subjects of other nations, longing for the Son of David to come, the one who was supposed to rule forever, and for the kingdom to be restored. And just like their ancestors, their hearts were prone to wander. Despite God's faithfulness to return them to their home, they kept looking elsewhere for their help and satisfaction.

So God sent one final prophet, Malachi, with a message of both hope and warning.

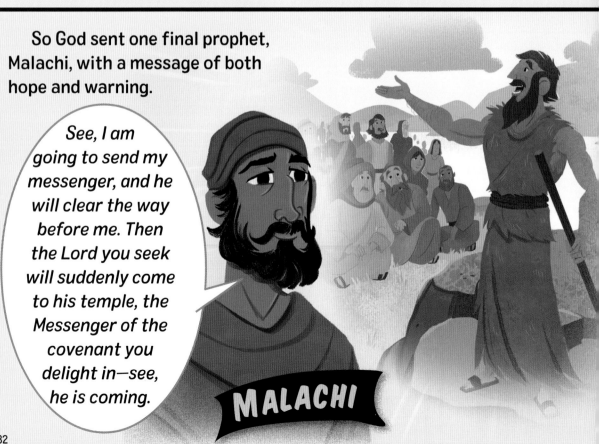

See, I am going to send my messenger, and he will clear the way before me. Then the Lord you seek will suddenly come to his temple, the Messenger of the covenant you delight in—see, he is coming.

MALACHI

And then God was silent.

No more prophets were sent. No visions. No signs or wonders.

Until four hundred years later, when an angel appeared to an elderly priest named Zechariah while he worked in the temple and gave him good news.

The One the people had waited for centuries was coming. The Promised Rescuer, the Son of David, the Offspring of Abraham, the Child of Eve.

God Himself.

But first, another would come. A forerunner, the messenger Malachi promised, who would cry out: "Prepare the way of the Lord in the wilderness; make a straight highway for our God in the desert."

And this priest, Zechariah himself, would be his father.

HOW CAN WE TRUST THAT GOD IS WORKING TO FULFILL HIS PLANS AND PROMISES EVEN WHEN HE SEEMS SILENT?

"I AM NOT THE MESSIAH"

For four hundred years, God had been silent. The people waited, remembering the words of the prophets. A Rescuer, the Messiah, was coming. He would restore the kingdom and remove their disgrace.

But four hundred years was a long time to wait. And some wondered, *Will this promise from God ever come true?*

Zechariah had another desire on his heart as he prayed in the temple. He and his wife, Elizabeth, longed for a child. But in all their years of marriage it had never happened.

THEN THE ANGEL APPEARED.

DO NOT BE AFRAID, BECAUSE YOUR PRAYER HAS BEEN HEARD. YOUR WIFE WILL BEAR YOU A SON AND YOU WILL NAME HIM JOHN.

HE WILL BE GREAT IN THE SIGHT OF THE LORD AND FILLED WITH THE HOLY SPIRIT WHILE STILL IN HIS MOTHER'S WOMB. HE WILL TURN MANY OF THE CHILDREN OF ISRAEL TO THE LORD THEIR GOD.

AND HE WILL GO BEFORE HIM IN THE SPIRIT AND POWER OF ELIJAH, TO MAKE READY FOR THE LORD A PREPARED PEOPLE.

Zechariah was amazed, but he didn't believe it. He was an old man and his wife was well past being able to have a baby. Because of Zechariah's unbelief, Gabriel made him silent until the birth of the child came to pass.

Soon, Elizabeth became pregnant. She rejoiced because God had looked on her with favor. And when the time came for her to give birth, she had a son, just as the angel had said. Her neighbors rejoiced, and when the time came to name the baby, these neighbors planned to call him Zechariah after his father.

The people were confused. No one in their family had that name. So they turned to Zechariah. He took a writing tablet and wrote, "His name is John."

Immediately Zechariah's mouth opened and he began to speak, praising God. All were amazed, but they wondered, *What will this child become?*

Many years passed. John grew into a man who wore a camel-hair tunic and a leather belt. This was the clothing of a prophet. He ministered near the Jordan River, calling God's people to turn away from their sins and be baptized to show their need and desire for God's forgiveness. Many came to him who were weighed down by their sins. But others came as well—religious leaders who relied on their heritage as descendants of Abraham to justify themselves and put demands on others that even they could not keep.

Produce fruit consistent with repentance! Don't start saying to yourselves, "We have Abraham as our father," for I tell you that God is able to raise up children for Abraham from these stones. The axe is already at the root of the trees. Therefore, every tree that doesn't produce good fruit will be cut down and thrown into the fire.

He told the crowds what this fruit looked like: Give to others who are in need. Don't cheat one another. Don't take advantage of people and abuse power.

John proclaimed good news to all the people. More came to see him and be baptized. He was popular among the people, but the religious leaders and officials despised him, especially King Herod.

The people wondered whether John might be the promised Rescuer, the Messiah who would restore the kingdom.

But John was not the Messiah, the promised Rescuer. He was the one who prepared the way for Him.

The Messiah was coming. Actually, He was already there. And soon He would make Himself known. But He would not be what anyone expected.

Matthew 1–2; Luke 1–2; Isaiah 7:14

GOOD NEWS OF GREAT JOY

From the day the angel visited her, Mary began to hold on to certain important moments, to store them up in her heart. She was a young girl, hardly the sort of person you would expect to be the mother of the Messiah. But an angel of the Lord, Gabriel, called her the favored one of God and told her all that would happen.

You will have a child by the Holy Spirit, and you are to name Him Jesus.

SEE, THE VIRGIN WILL BECOME PREGNANT AND GIVE BIRTH TO A SON, AND THEY WILL NAME HIM IMMANUEL...

She remembered the prophecy Isaiah had written down, more than seven hundred years before.

Immanuel—"God with us." Jesus—"God saves." When she told Joseph, the man she was soon to marry, he had a hard time believing it. *Could it really be true?*

He was a good man, and even though he thought she had been unfaithful to him, he didn't want others to shame Mary. To protect her, Joseph planned to break off their engagement quietly.

At least until Gabriel appeared to him too. The angel told him not to be afraid to take Mary as his wife.

This child is from the Holy Spirit. You will name Him Jesus, because He will save people from their sins.

Joseph told Mary what happened, and he promised to raise the child as his own.

After this, Mary went to stay with her cousin, Elizabeth.

Elizabeth was pregnant as well, and Mary had heard the stories of her husband, Zechariah, who was unable to speak after serving in the temple earlier that year. When Elizabeth saw her young relative, she was overjoyed—and the Holy Spirit filled her as her baby leaped inside her.

How could this happen to me, that the mother of my Lord should come to me? When the sound of your greeting reached my ears, the baby leaped for joy inside me!

Mary stayed with Elizabeth and Zechariah for several weeks before returning home.

As time passed, she heard people speaking about her in hushed tones. They whispered what they thought about how she came to be pregnant. Mary knew what was happening was impossible by human standards, but nothing is impossible for God.

Soon the time came for Mary and Joseph to travel to his ancestral home, Bethlehem, the home of King David, to be counted in a census.

Then the baby came. The only place for them to rest was among the animals, and it was there that her son came into the world.

The Son of God.

Immanuel, "God with us."

IMMANUEL— "GOD WITH US"

Shepherds arrived and told them of angels who had appeared and sung in the night sky, and how they were led to the baby by a bright star.

Then, when they took Jesus to be dedicated at the temple, an old man, Simeon, came and asked to hold the baby. His heart was filled with joy, and Simeon began to pray.

Simeon's words filled Mary with wonder. Her son was the Lord's salvation for His people.

Jesus: "God saves."

Now, Master, you can dismiss Your servant in peace, as You promised. For my eyes have seen Your salvation. You have prepared it in the presence of all peoples—a light for revelation to the Gentiles and glory to Your people Israel.

When the boy was two, they received visitors from another land. Wise men with gifts of gold, frankincense, and myrrh.

These were gifts fit for a King.

Is this the one born the king of the Jews? We have come to worship Him.

These men had seen the star that appeared in the sky the night Jesus was born. It was a sign that the king of the Jews, the Messiah, had been born. They traveled from their homeland in the east to Jerusalem, where they met with King Herod and his officials.

Herod was disturbed. He was appointed king by the Romans, but he was not a member of David's family. He was not even from the people of Israel—he was a descendant of Esau, Jacob's twin brother who sold his birthright for a meal. The throne did not belong to him. If a king from David's family were born, Herod would lose everything. He asked his chief priests where the Messiah would be born.

Tell me where you find the child so that I may worship him, too.

"Bethlehem," the priests said. *Of course*, he thought. *The city of David.*

Herod told the wise men to go to Bethlehem and asked them to return to Jerusalem when they found the King. "I wish to worship Him as well," he said.

When they found Jesus, they were warned in a dream not to return to Herod, and they returned home by a different road instead.

When Herod realized the wise men were not returning to him, he was furious. He sent soldiers to Bethlehem with orders to kill every male child two years old and younger.

Meanwhile, Joseph was warned in a dream to flee; so Mary, Joseph, and Jesus went to Egypt, where they stayed for about four years, until Herod's death.

When they returned to
Judea, they settled in Nazareth.

Jesus was a kind boy, obedient and thoughtful,
growing in wisdom, and full of God's grace, which made the next
event in His young life even stranger.

When He was twelve, His family went to Jerusalem to celebrate
the Passover. But when His family and their traveling companions
left to return to Galilee, Jesus stayed behind.

They had been travelling for a day,
before they realized He was missing.

His parents searched throughout the entire group, but He wasn't there. They turned back and returned to Jerusalem. It took them another three days to find Him; He was at the temple sitting with the teachers, listening and asking questions.

Son, why have You done this to us?

Why are you searching for Me? Didn't you know I needed to be in My Father's house?

They didn't understand what He meant by this. But all the teachers had marveled at Jesus's questions and understanding of the Scriptures. He returned home with them without difficulty, and as He grew, Jesus grew even more in wisdom and favor with God and with people.

All the events of His early life gave Mary much to consider as she tried to make sense of all she had seen. Her son was different from other children, including His brothers and sisters. He wasn't simply a boy. He was Something else. And years later, when she saw Him at the end of His ministry, hanging from a cross, it would all make sense:

He was the One God had been promising from the very beginning. He was the One who would crush the serpent's head. He was the King who would sit on David's throne. He was the Messiah, the promised Rescuer who would make all things new.

Immanuel, "God with us."

Jesus, the God who saves.

WHAT STEPS CAN YOU TAKE TO REMEMBER HOW GOD HAS BEEN AT WORK IN YOUR LIFE?

JESUS'S BAPTISM AND TEMPTATION

Before Jesus's ministry began, John was baptizing and preaching by the Jordan. When he saw Jesus, John cried "Look, the Lamb of God who takes away the sins of the world!"

This was the One he had been born to point God's people to.

Jesus was the One he had been waiting for, the One who would rescue and restore God's people.

Jesus was coming into the water. Asking to be baptized. A baptism He didn't need. Baptism was a symbol of repentance, of turning away from sin.

And Jesus had never sinned.

Why are You coming to me? I'm the one who should be baptized by You!

I know it seems strange but trust Me, this is the way it must happen to fulfill God's plan.

When Jesus came up out of the water, something incredible happened: the Spirit of God descended in the form of a dove, and rested upon Him. Then from out of the sky, there was a voice.

THIS IS MY BELOVED SON, IN WHOM I AM WELL-PLEASED.

After this, Jesus went into the wilderness where He remained for forty days and nights, fasting and praying. At the end of this time, He was hungry.

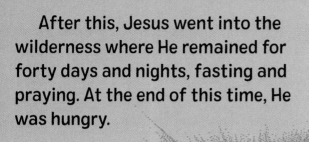
Then, the tempter—the devil—appeared to test Jesus.

If you are the Son of God, tell these stones to become bread.

It is written: Man must not live on bread alone but on every word that comes from the mouth of God.

Jesus *could* turn stones into bread, and He *was* hungry. But Jesus did not need to use His power for such a small thing. It was better that He remain hungry and obey God. His Father would provide what He needed in time.

Then the devil took Him to Jerusalem, to the very top of the temple. The devil said to Him, "If You are the Son of God, throw Yourself down. For it is written that He will give His angels orders concerning You . . . so that you will not strike Your foot against a stone."

Jesus replied as He had before, "It is also written: Do not test the Lord your God."

Even as he misused the words of Scripture, the devil was right: the Father loved His Son and did not wish to see Him come to harm. But Jesus knew that to test God in this way—to try and "make" a miracle happen—was really to call into question His goodness. It was a sign of unbelief.

Finally, the devil took Jesus to a very high mountain and showed Him all the kingdoms of the world, in all their beauty. Then the tempter made his final appeal.

I will give You all these — if You will fall down and worship me.

Go away, Satan! For it is written: Worship the Lord your God, and serve only Him.

The devil's final offer was one that would spare Jesus the cross, even as it gave Him authority over all the world. But it would mean worshiping one who is unworthy of worship: a created thing, and the enemy of God at that! To do such a thing was unthinkable. Jesus refused once again, and the devil left.

Before the temptation even began, Jesus understood His identity: He was the Son of God, with whom His Father was well-pleased. And when the devil tried to tempt Him, it was Jesus's identity that he was challenging with one word: if.

"If you are the Son of God . . ." the devil said. But Jesus knew there was no "if." He was the Son of God. The Son who was tempted but did not fall. The Son who stood in the place of His people so that by faith in Him, the Father would say to them, "This is My beloved son, and this is my beloved daughter. With them, I am well-pleased."

JESUS WAS TEMPTED IN EVERY WAY WE ARE. HOW DOES IT HELP US TO KNOW THAT JESUS WAS TEMPTED TOO?

Matthew 4, 10; Luke 4

"COME, FOLLOW ME"

Jesus walked along the Sea of Galilee and saw Simon Peter and Andrew throwing a net from their fishing boat. These would be the first He would call to be His disciples. The next were fishermen like them—James and John, the sons of Zebedee. When they heard the call, they immediately dropped their nets, leaped from their boats, and followed Him as soon as they reached the shore. Fishermen would become fishers of men.

Come, follow Me!

Then came Philip, Bartholomew, and Thomas. Then Jesus met Matthew, also called Levi, who was a tax collector. Jesus saw him and gave the same command, "Follow Me." Matthew left his toll booth behind and went with Jesus. Then James, Thaddeus, Simon the Zealot, and finally Judas Iscariot, the one who would betray Him.

These were the Twelve. Fishermen, a tax collector, and even a rebel! Hardly the kind of people anyone would expect the Messiah to choose as His disciples.

Which was exactly the point.

From the beginning, God used unlikely people to carry out His plan of salvation:

An old man to be the father of a great nation.

A resented brother to rescue his family.

A young boy to defeat a giant.

A young girl to be the mother of the Messiah.

Through His twelve disciples, Jesus would bring the good news of the gospel to the ends of the earth. They were not among the elite and highly educated. They were ordinary people who knew of their own need for a Savior.

God still does this today as the gospel spreads: He uses ordinary people who feel the weight of their sin, who recognize their need of a Savior, to share the good news of what God has done. And He will keep doing this until the day there is no one left to hear this good news, and when all of us who are sick with sin are healed and made whole once more.

DO YOU FEEL UNEQUIPPED TO SHARE THE GOSPEL? HOW DOES THIS STORY ENCOURAGE YOU?

A TEACHER WITH AUTHORITY

When Jesus began to teach, people didn't know what to do with Him. He was not like the other teachers they heard. Jesus was different; He was special. But what made Him special wasn't a special style of speaking; it was because He had real authority from God.

Jesus's teaching challenged everyone who heard it, even as it gave hope to those who longed for the coming of the kingdom of God. He taught that those who are the poor in spirit, the humble who mourn over their sin, and those who desire righteousness are blessed. The kingdom of God belongs to them, and they will enjoy peace with God.

Blessed are the poor in spirit, for the kingdom of heaven is theirs.

God's people were the light of the world, He said. "Don't hide your light under a basket . . . let your light shine before others, so that they may see your good works and give glory to your Father in heaven."

When you give to the poor, don't let your right hand know what the left is doing. Your Father who sees in secret will reward you.

He said that God is not honored through giving that draws attention to the giver, nor does He answer the prayers of the one who prays to be seen. Those who do these things are hypocrites. Instead, God wants His people to give and pray with a quiet and humble spirit.

As Jesus taught His people to pray, He gave a model for them to follow, one that taught them to put God first in all things—to pursue His holiness and His will, as they live in gratitude for all He has done for them.

Don't babble as you pray, as if more words are better words. Your Father knows what you need before you even ask.

When you pray, pray like this:

OUR FATHER IN HEAVEN,
YOUR NAME BE HONORED AS HOLY.
YOUR KINGDOM COME.
YOUR WILL BE DONE
ON EARTH AS IT IS IN HEAVEN.
GIVE US TODAY OUR DAILY BREAD.
AND FORGIVE US OUR DEBTS,
AS WE ALSO HAVE FORGIVEN OUR DEBTORS.
AND DO NOT BRING US INTO TEMPTATION,
BUT DELIVER US FROM THE EVIL ONE.

He warned the people of the dangers of outwardly obeying God's commands while breaking them in their hearts. He warned that hate is as bad as murder, and desiring what doesn't belong to you is as bad as stealing it.

He told them that it was better not to make oaths or promises, but simply to say yes or no honestly and to give to anyone who asks of them. He said to do good to all who meant them harm, to not only love their neighbor but also their enemy. Just as God shows compassion to the righteous and unrighteous alike, sending the sun and rain to both, Jesus said, "Love your enemies and pray for those who persecute you so that you may be children of your Father in heaven."

They were not to collect treasures on earth, gaining great wealth in this world while neglecting the things of God. The love of money and possessions is a trap, because they don't last. Only the kingdom of God lasts forever, so seek God's kingdom first, and He will provide all that you need.

Jesus warned the people to choose carefully what they built their lives on. Some were like those who built their houses on a rock. When the storms came and the rain fell, their houses stood firm. Others were like those who built their houses on the sand. When the storms came and the rain fell, their houses collapsed.

Jesus wanted them to understand that they had a choice to make between Himself and any other foundation for living. Jesus Himself was the rock in this story, and a life with Him as its foundation would stand up to the "storms" of life—the difficulties and temptations they faced each day, and, ultimately, the judgment of God. The "house" would stand because it had a strong foundation.

But people could choose another foundation, one focused on doing good works—even things God says His people should do like giving money to people who need help, being kind to others, and even praying regularly! But trying to please God through good behavior alone is like building a house on a foundation of sand. When the storms come, it cannot stand.

Therefore, everyone who hears these words of mine and acts on them will be like a wise man who built his house on the rock.

Jesus taught all these things and much more. Many who heard Him believed and followed Him. But others were filled with confusion—and even anger—especially when He taught about the Messiah, the promised Rescuer of God's people.

When Jesus spoke in the synagogue in Nazareth, He read from the scroll of Isaiah. The passage was a prophecy about the Messiah, God's promised Rescuer from the family of David. Isaiah wrote that the Messiah would preach good news to the poor, proclaim release to captives and recovery of sight to the blind, set free the oppressed, and proclaim the year of the Lord's favor. When He finished reading, Jesus rolled up the scroll and sat down. The people looked at Him, waiting for Him to explain what He read.

"This Scripture is fulfilled," was all He said. Many were amazed, but some were skeptical. *This was Joseph's son*, they thought. *Could He be saying that He is the Messiah?*

Jesus condemned their unbelief, reminding them that they were following in the footsteps of their ancestors. The crowd was furious and tried to drive Jesus off a cliff. Somehow, He slipped away and walked through the crowd unnoticed.

When thousands came to Him looking for food to eat, Jesus told them He was the bread of life, the bread that the manna in the desert pointed forward to. No one who came to Him would be hungry again.

Truly I tell you, anyone who believes has eternal life. I am the bread of life . . . . I am the living bread that came down from heaven. If anyone eats of this bread he will live forever. The bread that I will give for the life of the world is My flesh.

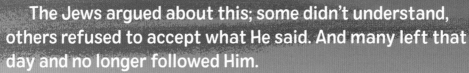

The Jews argued about this; some didn't understand, others refused to accept what He said. And many left that day and no longer followed Him.

But Jesus needed to teach these truths. He needed to tell them all these things. This was, after all, what a good shepherd did.

And Jesus is the Good Shepherd. He knows His flock by name and leads them to green pastures. He gives them all that they need and renews their lives, leading them along the right paths for His name's sake. Jesus is the Good Shepherd who lays down His life for the sheep.

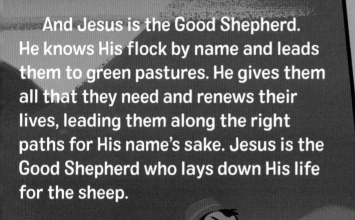

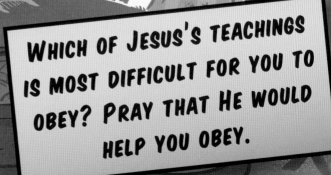

WHICH OF JESUS'S TEACHINGS IS MOST DIFFICULT FOR YOU TO OBEY? PRAY THAT HE WOULD HELP YOU OBEY.

"THE KINGDOM OF HEAVEN IS LIKE..."

During Jesus' ministry, He taught the people many important truths about God and His kingdom. He wanted to tell them about what the kingdom is like and what God expects of His people. Sometimes He taught the people plainly, as He did during the Sermon on the Mount. But other times He taught people using parables, or stories.

Many began with the words, "The kingdom of heaven is like . . ."

The kingdom of heaven is like a treasure buried in a field: a man found it and reburied it, and sold everything he owned to buy the field. His point was that the kingdom is worth more than any-thing else—when we find it, we must give all we have to receive it.

Another parable began with a sower, or farmer. As he cast seed, some of it fell on the hard path and was devoured by birds. Some fell in rocky ground, sprouted quickly, and was scorched by the sun because it had no root. Some fell among the weeds and was choked to death. But some fell on good soil and grew into strong plants that bore much fruit, some a hundred, others sixty, and others still thirty times the amount of seed sown.

The seed was the Word of God, the sower was the preacher, and the ground was the hearts of the hearers. Some had hearts that were like the hard path; they rejected the Word outright. Others had hearts like the rocky ground and received the Word with joy, but it didn't last. Still others had hearts so filled up with the cares of the world that the Word couldn't grow. But some hearts were like good soil. They weren't better than any of the others, but their hearts were more receptive. Because of it, the Word bore fruit.

PAY ME **ALL** THAT YOU OWE!

Some parables were meant to challenge the attitudes of their hearers. Jesus told about an unmerciful servant who had been forgiven a great debt. He had gone to his master and begged forgiveness, and out of compassion, the master forgave the loan and released him. Then the servant approached another man who owed him a small debt. This man made the same plea for mercy as the servant, but unlike his master, the servant was unmerciful.

He refused to forgive the loan and had the man thrown in prison. When his master heard, he had the wicked servant thrown in prison until his debt could be paid.

THOSE WHO HAVE BEEN FORGIVEN MUCH MUST ALSO FORGIVE; FORGIVEN PEOPLE FORGIVE.

In the parable of the good Samaritan, Jesus rebuked the religious leaders who tried to put limits on God's commands to love their neighbors as themselves. In this story, a man had been beaten, robbed, and left for dead. A priest saw him and crossed on the other side of the road. A teacher of the Law did the same. The only person who stopped was a Samaritan. The Jews hated the Samaritans, who were descendants of the tribes that made up the Northern

Kingdom of Israel but did not worship God as they did. But this Samaritan did something that no other traveler did: He helped the beaten man. He took him to an inn and paid for his care.

He showed compassion when no one else did.

229

In the parable of the talents, Jesus spoke of three servants who were each given a sum of money by their master to invest, each according to his ability. When the master asked what had become of the money given to them, two servants had doubled their money.

The master said to both of them, "Well done, good and faithful servant! You were faithful over a few things; I will put you in charge of many things. Share your master's joy."

But the third servant came to his master with only the money he had been given in his hands. He explained that he knew that has master was harsh, so he buried it, afraid of losing it. The master was furious and demanded to know why, if he was so harsh a master, the servant did not at least put the money in the bank to collect interest! Then he punished the servant for his unfaithfulness.

But the best known of the parables follows two others that make the same point.

First, He told a story about a shepherd who left his ninety-nine sheep behind to find the one that was lost, and when he found it, he rejoiced.

Then came a story about a woman who searched all throughout her home for a lost coin, and when she found it, she rejoiced.

And finally the story about a father who had two sons, the obedient elder son and the foolish younger son. The younger son went to his father and demanded his inheritance. The father gave it to him, and the son went to a faraway land. There, he spent the money on wild living.

But when the money was all gone, he was lost.

THE PIGS EAT BETTER THAN ME!!

When he realized how foolish he had been, the younger son returned home to ask to be treated as a hired servant of his father.

But when the father saw his son coming, he gathered some robes and ran to the son. The father threw his arms around the young man and welcomed him home before announcing a great celebration in honor of the one who was lost, but was now found.

But here's where the story was different from the others: there was another son, another who was lost. The elder son who had remained with his father and worked his fields could not bring himself to rejoice in his brother's return. And the story ended in an unspoken question:

WILL YOU COME AND REJOICE TOO?

The question in the parable was a plea to Jesus's hearers. The Pharisees were furious because sinners and tax collectors—the disreputable in society—were flocking to Jesus. The Pharisees were rejecting what God was doing. All of heaven rejoiced when one lost sinner repented, but the religious leaders could not. And what they revealed about themselves is that they too were lost.

They could not share in their master's joy because they saw Him as a harsh man. They were squandering what had been entrusted to them. Their hearts were hard, and the Word was being snatched away before it even had a chance to take root.

But Jesus comes for all His lost sheep, even those who think they're already found. And when He finds them, He will rejoice—and all of heaven will too.

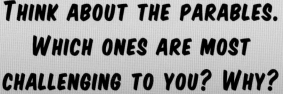

THINK ABOUT THE PARABLES. WHICH ONES ARE MOST CHALLENGING TO YOU? WHY?

"WHAT KIND OF MAN IS THIS?"

The waves crashed around the boat. The disciples were experienced fishermen, and the Sea of Galilee was familiar to them, but they had never experienced anything like this. Water was filling the boat faster than they could bail it back out over the sides.

Meanwhile,
Jesus was asleep.

LORD, SAVE US! *We're going to die!*

Jesus woke up, and got to His feet, His eyes still blurry from His sleep. He looked on as the waves crashed against the sides of their boat, and He heard the splintering of wood. Then He spoke to His disciples.

Then He turned again to the winds and the waves, and with a word they stopped. The water was completely still. A greater terror gripped the disciples' hearts. *What kind of man is this,* they wondered, *that even the winds and sea obeyed Him?*

This was not the first time they had asked this question, nor would it be the last. Throughout His ministry, there were many moments like this one, when Jesus did something that shouldn't have been possible: He performed signs and wonders. He performed miracles.

The first time anyone saw Him perform a miracle was at a wedding in Cana. Everyone was celebrating when the wine ran out. His mother told Him what had happened and took Jesus to the servants. He told them to pour water into six stone jars, each holding twenty or thirty gallons. The servants did as Jesus said. The headwaiter tasted it and was amazed. And when the groom had tasted it, he was even more pleased. Normally at this point in the celebration, the wine was poor quality—but this was the best offering in the entire wedding!

This miracle was a sign revealing Jesus's identity as the Messiah. But it was only the first.

Take some to the headwaiter.

Jesus was preaching in Capernaum and a great crowd gathered around the house where He taught. Four men brought their paralyzed friend to Him but couldn't get through the door. So they climbed up onto the roof, opened a space, and lowered him down to Jesus.

When Jesus saw him, He said, "Your sins are forgiven."

The religious leaders in the crowd were shocked at this.

How could Jesus, a human being, say this? This was blasphemy! Only God could forgive sins. But Jesus knew what they were thinking.

Why are you thinking these things in your hearts? Which is easier: to say to this man, "Your sins are forgiven," or to say, "Get up, take your mat, and walk"?

But so that you may know that the Son of Man has authority on earth to forgive sins, I tell you: get up, take your mat, and go home.

Immediately, the man got up, took his mat and went home, and many who saw rejoiced.

Jesus healed many others as well. He healed the blind and the lame, the sick and the infirm. Everywhere He went, people came asking for His help, and He gladly gave it.

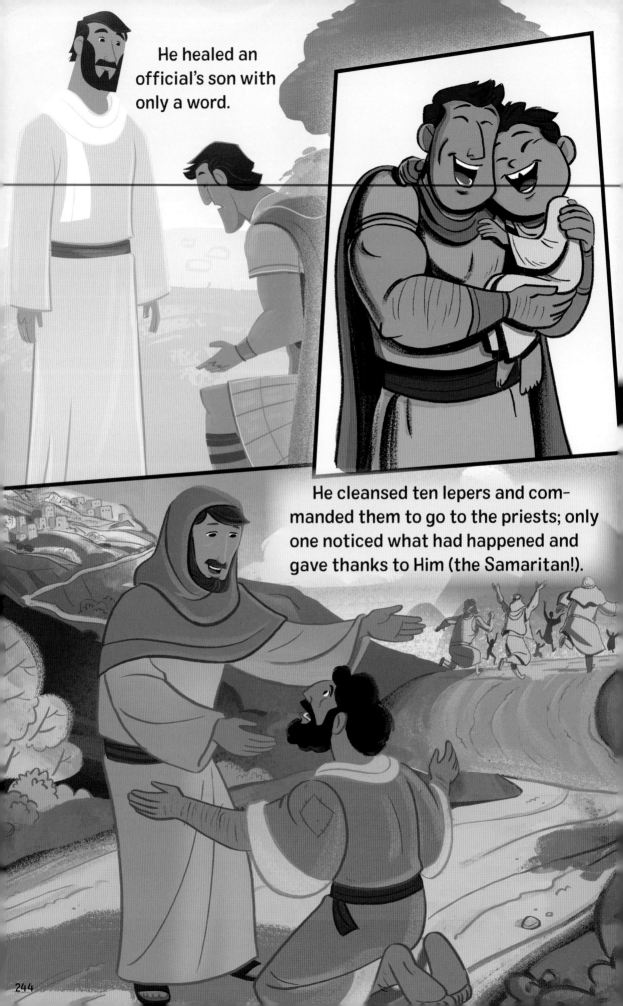

He healed an official's son with only a word.

He cleansed ten lepers and commanded them to go to the priests; only one noticed what had happened and gave thanks to Him (the Samaritan!).

He healed a woman with an illness that made her bleed for more than twelve years simply through her touching His robes while He was on His way to restore a young girl who had died.

I AM HEALED!

He even healed people who were troubled by evil spirits. When Jesus went to the region of the Gerasenes, He met a man who lived in the tombs. The man had a wild look in his eyes. His clothes were tattered, and he had chains around his arms. And when the man spoke, it was not with a human voice.

AND IT WAS FILLED WITH FEAR.

LEGION BECAUSE WE ARE MANY!

What is your name?

As Jesus commanded the spirits to leave the man, they saw a herd of pigs nearby. Legion begged Jesus to be sent into the pigs. Jesus agreed, and as the spirits entered them, the pigs ran off and down a cliff to drown in the sea.

The man who had been tormented returned to his village to share what Jesus had done. But the men who tended the pigs saw what happened and were frightened of Jesus, this Man with power over evil.

Jesus performed other signs as well, including showing that He had the ability to provide for all His people's needs.

After a long day of teaching, He saw that the crowd, which numbered five thousand men plus women and children, were hungry. The disciples encouraged Him to dismiss them so they could go and eat, but Jesus had a better idea.

You give them something to eat.

What can we give them? It would take more money than we could earn in two hundred days to feed them all!

Jesus asked about what food they had. It was five small loaves of bread and two fish. Enough for a young boy's lunch. They brought Jesus the food. He blessed it and commanded His disciples to distribute it to all the people. Everyone had as much as they could eat, and when they were done there were twelve baskets of leftovers—one for each of Jesus's disciples.

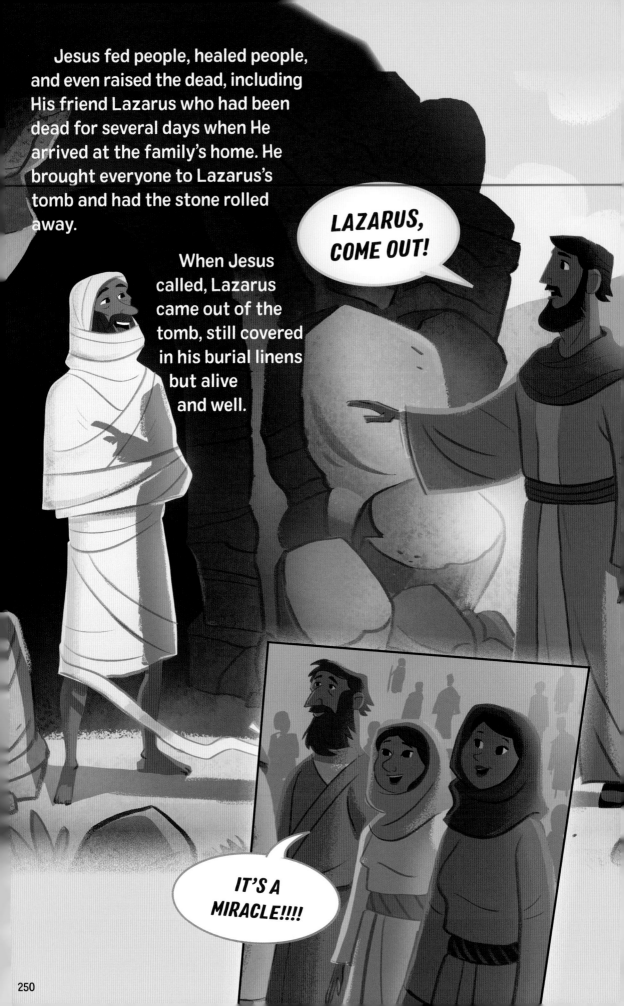

Jesus fed people, healed people, and even raised the dead, including His friend Lazarus who had been dead for several days when He arrived at the family's home. He brought everyone to Lazarus's tomb and had the stone rolled away.

When Jesus called, Lazarus came out of the tomb, still covered in his burial linens but alive and well.

LAZARUS, COME OUT!

IT'S A MIRACLE!!!!

But perhaps the most amaz-ing miracle of all was one that was seen by only three men: Peter, James, and John, the men closest to Jesus among His disciples. He took the three of them to the top of a mountain, and there He revealed His glory. His face shone like the sun, and His clothes became dazzling white, as if they were made of light. And two men appeared beside Jesus, Moses, and Elijah, and spoke with Him. And then there was a voice from the heavens.

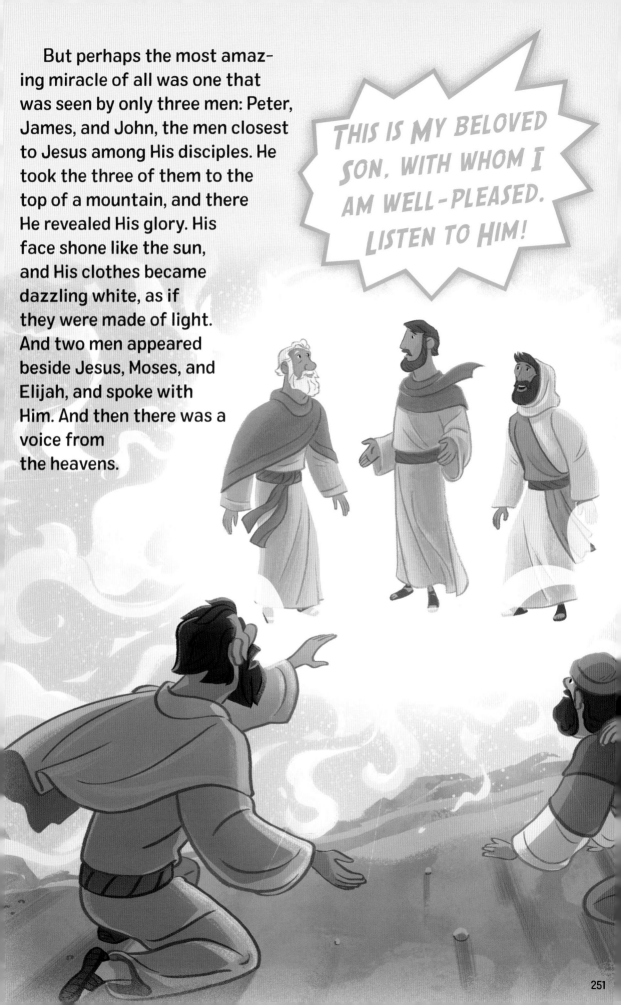

THIS IS MY BELOVED SON, WITH WHOM I AM WELL-PLEASED. LISTEN TO HIM!

They fell down in fear, and when they looked up, everything was normal. Jesus looked the way He had before. But their entire world had changed.

In this sign, as He had been doing with every sign and wonder He did, Jesus revealed Himself to be the One they had been waiting for—the One all God's people had been waiting for since the moment God had cast the first people out of the garden. He was the Messiah, the promised Rescuer.

Deliverance was coming soon. Sin would be defeated. The serpent would be crushed. But victory would be costly.

HOW DO THE MIRACLES OF JESUS HELP YOU TO BELIEVE THAT HE IS THE MESSIAH?

Matthew 21; Luke 21–22; John 12

"HOSANNA!"

Why are you bothering this woman? She has done a noble thing for Me . . . She has prepared Me for burial. Truly I tell you, wherever this gospel is proclaimed in the whole world, what she has done will also be told in memory of her.

The disciples were confused. A woman had come into the room while they were eating, holding an alabaster jar filled with expensive perfume.

Instead of offering it as a gift, she poured it over Jesus's head—and then she started to wash His feet with her hair. And He said this was a *good* thing? If the perfume had been sold, it could have blessed the poor. But now it had been wasted. And the woman . . . She had embarrassed herself, but Jesus was saying that this would be spoken of anywhere the gospel was proclaimed?

They didn't understand. They were with Jesus every day for years, and they still missed what He was teaching them. They knew He was the One God sent into the world to preach good news. They knew He was the Messiah, the promised Rescuer of God's people. But they didn't know what that meant. Not really. And it would only get more confusing in the days to come.

Jesus and His disciples made the journey from Bethany to Jerusalem. Jesus sent two of the disciples ahead to a village, where they were to speak with a man and get a young donkey, one that had never been ridden before. Jesus rode the donkey into the city, His disciples laying down their cloaks and leafy branches along the ground. And all who came before and after Him rejoiced.

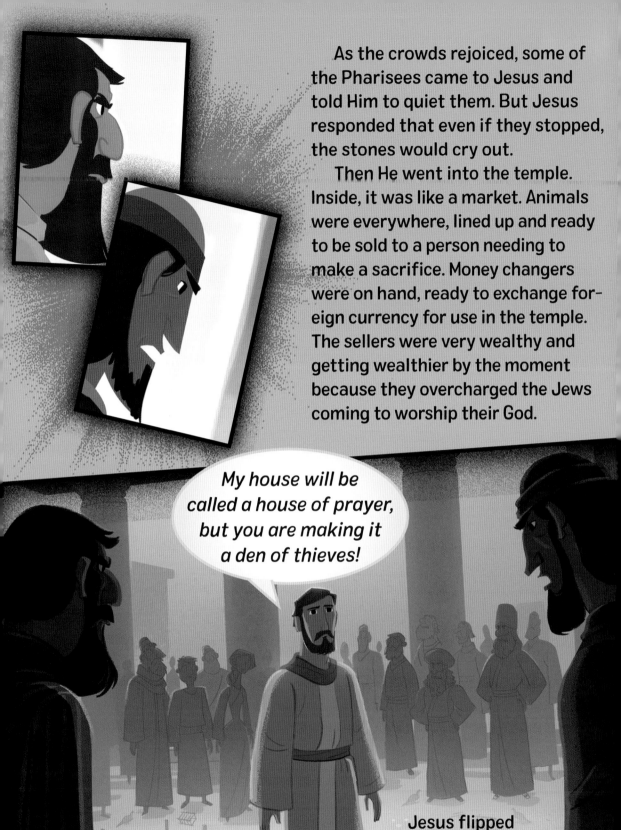

As the crowds rejoiced, some of the Pharisees came to Jesus and told Him to quiet them. But Jesus responded that even if they stopped, the stones would cry out.

Then He went into the temple. Inside, it was like a market. Animals were everywhere, lined up and ready to be sold to a person needing to make a sacrifice. Money changers were on hand, ready to exchange foreign currency for use in the temple. The sellers were very wealthy and getting wealthier by the moment because they overcharged the Jews coming to worship their God.

My house will be called a house of prayer, but you are making it a den of thieves!

Jesus flipped over their tables and chased the money changers out of the temple with a whip!

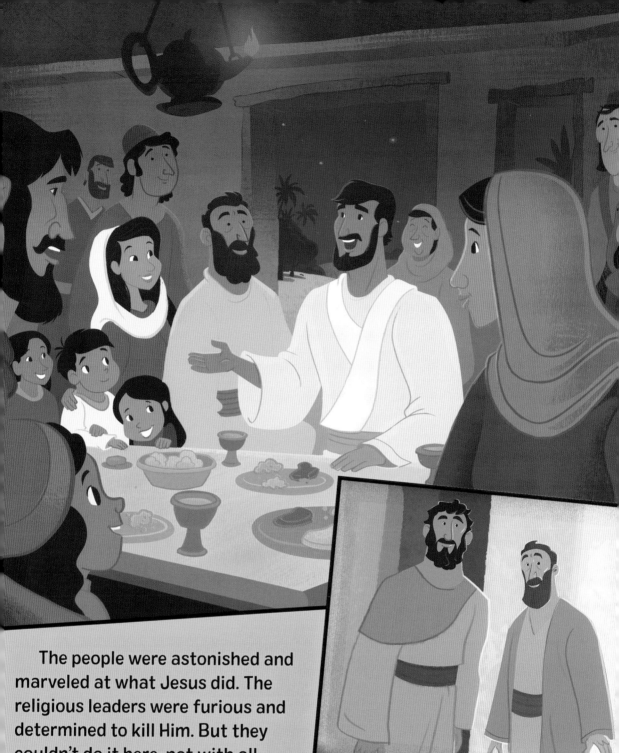

The people were astonished and marveled at what Jesus did. The religious leaders were furious and determined to kill Him. But they couldn't do it here, not with all the people around Him. Jesus was too popular. The people loved Him. Moving against Him here would cause a riot.

They had to wait until an opportunity presented itself. And they wouldn't have to wait long.

From the moment Jesus's disciples realized He was the Messiah, He had begun to tell them of what was to happen: He would go to Jerusalem, be handed over to the religious leaders, and be killed. But they didn't understand this. They couldn't imagine a Messiah who had to die—or that any of *them* would play a part in it happening.

But Judas Iscariot was a thief and was stealing money from the group. He was the one who became angry when the woman poured the perfume over Jesus's head. He couldn't see her act of worship. He only saw the money disappear as the perfume poured over Jesus. He went to the religious leaders and agreed to betray Jesus in exchange for thirty pieces of silver.

But he couldn't do it immediately. He had to wait for the right moment.

But he, like the religious leaders, wouldn't have to wait long.

GOD USES ALL THINGS FOR HIS GLORY AND OUR GOOD, EVEN ACTS AS TERRIBLE AS JUDAS PLANNING TO BETRAY JESUS. HOW DOES KNOWING THIS HELP US TRUST GOD DURING DIFFICULT TIMES IN OUR LIVES?

Matthew 26–27; Luke 22–23; John 18–19

"ARE YOU THE CHRIST?"

Jesus's disciples were stunned. They were celebrating the Passover meal, eaten in remembrance of the Israelites' escape from Egypt so many centuries before, when Jesus told them that one of them would betray Him.

> Surely not I, Rabbi?

> Truly I tell you, one of you will betray Me. The one who dips his hand with Me in the bowl—he will betray Me.

The bowl came to Judas Iscariot who dipped his hand into the bowl. He then got up and left the disciples.

No one seemed to notice.

Then, Jesus took the bread, blessed it, broke it, and gave it to His disciples.

Take and eat it; this is My body.

Then he took a cup, and gave thanks before giving it to them.

Drink from it, all of you. For this is My blood of the covenant, which is poured out for many for the forgiveness of sins.

Then the disciples sang a hymn, and went to the garden of Gethsemane.

In the garden, Jesus asked the disciples to sit and pray for Him while He went to pray alone. His steps were as heavy as His heart. He fell to His knees and prayed.

My Father, if it is possible, let this cup pass from me. Yet not as I will, but Your will be done.

Jesus knew what was coming. The "cup" was being passed to Him, and by taking it, Jesus was going to experience God's holy anger at sin. He was about to be betrayed, arrested, and killed in the place of sinners. But was there some other way for God to forgive sinners—could forgiveness come by some other means?

An angel appeared from heaven, sent by the Father to strengthen Jesus. This was God's answer: there was no other way.

After each time He prayed, Jesus rose and went back to the disciples and found them asleep. Each time He asked them to stay awake and pray, but they kept being overcome by weariness.

Suddenly, a mob arrived, swords and clubs in hand, with the religious leaders and teachers of the Law. And in the lead was Judas Iscariot. The religious leaders arrested Jesus and took Him to stand before the Sanhedrin.

Standing before an angry crowd, the high priest asked Jesus if He was the Son of God.

The high priest was enraged and tore his robes, declaring Jesus guilty of blasphemy. Then the crowd began to spit on Him and beat him. They took Him to Pilate, who questioned Him for a long time, despite his wife saying that Pilate should have nothing to do with this man.

He found Jesus had done nothing wrong—but Pilate feared the people. He had Jesus beaten and said this was enough. Jesus should be released—but the people would not listen.

"CRUCIFY! CRUCIFY HIM!" they cried.

Seeing the people would not be convinced, Pilate handed Jesus over. He was led away and made to carry a wooden cross to the place outside the city called the Skull. A crowd followed Him as He walked, some mocking Him, but others mourned and cried out in sorrow.

In the garden, He had prayed that the cup—God's holy anger at sin—would pass from Him. But it remained His to drink. So He did. As He was led through the streets of Jerusalem, it was as a lamb led to the slaughter. As the nails were driven through His hands and feet, He was pierced because of our rebellion. As He was beaten, He was crushed because of our sins.

He was the Lamb that would take away the sins of the world, who demonstrated the greatest love of all—giving His life for His friends. And through His sacrifice, all who trust in Him are healed.

HOW CAN YOU LIVE DIFFERENTLY TODAY BECAUSE OF JESUS'S SACRIFICE?

"IT IS FINISHED"

IF YOU ARE THE SON OF GOD, COME DOWN FROM THE CROSS! COME DOWN AND WE WILL BELIEVE!

The crowd mocked Jesus as He hung on the cross between two thieves. They said that if He was the King of the Jews, He should come down. *Then* they would believe.

But Jesus would not come down. He could not. His work was not yet complete. He listened as the people mocked and jeered, but He did not respond. He only prayed,

"Father, forgive them because they do not know what they are doing."

He remained on the cross. His work was not yet complete.

The day went on. At about noon, the sky became as dark as night, as if the sun had gone out. But Jesus remained on the cross. His work was not yet complete.

Around three in the afternoon, the sun returned and the earth shook. And from the cross, Jesus cried out

IT IS FINISHED!

The people were terrified. *What* was finished? Jesus's breath was shallow, and, using the last of His strength, He said, "Father, into your hands I entrust My spirit."

Then He breathed His last. As He did, the curtain in the temple split in two and revealed the Most Holy Place.

When the soldiers saw Jesus was not breathing, they stabbed Him in the side with a spear. Water and blood poured from the wound in His side. There was no doubt: Jesus was dead.

Jesus's body was taken down from the cross. His disciples wrapped His body in linen cloths and placed Him in a newly cut tomb. A stone was rolled in front of the entrance, and it was sealed. The religious leaders placed guards at its entrance in case anyone tried to take His body.

Jesus's work was complete. The payment for sin had been made. He was dead. His body rested in the tomb. But He would not stay there. On the cross, He had willingly laid down His life for those He loved, for everyone who would believe in Him.

Soon, He would take it up again.

WHY IS JESUS'S DEATH CALLED "GOOD NEWS"?

Matthew 28; Luke 24; John 20

"HE IS NOT HERE"

She couldn't believe it! The man she thought was a gardener—it was Jesus. Earlier that morning, she had gone to the tomb, but the stone had already been rolled away, and His body was gone. She'd run to tell the disciples what had happened, and Peter had raced to the tomb. All he had found were the linens Jesus had been wrapped in. Peter had gone back to where the disciples were staying, but she had stayed behind and wept.

BUT NOW, HE WAS HERE!

272

Two of the disciples were walking toward Emmaus and speaking of all that had happened, when Jesus joined them. They could not recognize Him.

Then beginning with Moses and all the prophets, He interpreted for them the things concerning Himself in all the Scriptures. He then stopped to share a meal with them. As He gave thanks and broke the bread, the two realized He was Jesus. Then Jesus disappeared, and the two disciples raced back to Jerusalem, eager to tell the others the good news: *JESUS WAS ALIVE!*

That evening, as the disciples were hiding in a locked room, Jesus appeared among them.

After eating some broiled fish, Jesus disappeared again. But He kept reappearing. One day, as some of the other disciples were fishing, Jesus appeared on the shore. He called to the disciples, and Peter jumped from the boat to see Jesus. On the shore, Peter saw a fire with fish and bread being cooked over it.

"Come and eat," Jesus said.

After they ate, Jesus turned to Peter and asked, "Do you love Me?"

Peter was nervous, and with good reason. Before Jesus was arrested, Peter swore that even if everyone else turned away from Him, Peter would not abandon Him. "Even if I must die, I won't deny you," Peter boasted. But when Jesus actually *was* arrested, Peter denied being one of Jesus's disciples when questioned by a servant girl.

Will Jesus now deny me like I denied Him? he wondered. But instead of denying Peter, Jesus *restored* him to his role as one of Jesus's disciples.

Jesus also appeared to Thomas, the one who doubted, and allowed him to touch the holes in His hands and side. Jesus appeared again and again to individuals and to large groups, as many as five hundred people at one time.

JESUS WAS ALIVE.

He was the Messiah—the Rescuer God had promised would come. Death could not hold Him. He had defeated it.

DO YOU FIND IT HARD TO BELIEVE THAT THE RESURRECTION REALLY HAPPENED? WHY OR WHY NOT?

But He would not stay. Soon, He had to go to the Father—to sit on the throne long ago promised to His ancestor David, and rule over all creation as its King. And when He did, He would entrust His disciples with the good news that changes everything.

GO INTO ALL THE WORLD

For forty days after His resurrection, Jesus had been with the disciples. In private and in public, He met with them, teaching, encouraging, and strengthening them for what lay ahead. The time had come for Him to return to the Father and sit on His throne, ruling over all the world forever and ever.

So the disciples traveled to Galilee from Jerusalem, to a mountain. They saw Jesus there on the mountain and worshiped Him. But Peter wanted to know something important.

Lord, when are you restoring the kingdom to Israel?

It is not for you to know times or periods that the Father has set by His own authority.

Go and make disciples of all nations, baptizing them in the name of the Father and of the Son and of the Holy Spirit, teaching them to observe everything I have commanded you. And remember, I am with you always, to the end of the age.

The disciples were confused. They still did not understand, not fully. The kingdom of God was not what they expected. It was not like a kingdom made by human beings. It was a kingdom that would spread through the disciples as they told people about Jesus.

"But," Jesus said, "you must wait." Before they could begin their mission, Jesus was going to send them a helper—the Holy Spirit. "When the Holy Spirit comes, you will have power."

The disciples wanted to ask more questions. When would the Holy Spirit come? How would they know?

279

But before they could ask, Jesus began to rise up from the ground into the sky. The disciples were amazed as they watched Jesus rise higher and higher. Then a cloud took Him out of their sight, and He was gone.

The disciples continued to stare into the sky, unsure of what to do next. Suddenly two men in white clothes appeared in their midst.

Why are you standing here looking up into heaven? Jesus will return in the same way you have seen Him go.

The disciples left and returned to Jerusalem, still unsure of what to make of all Jesus had said but trusting that what He said would come true. When they arrived, they went to the upper room of the house where they were staying to pray.

More believers joined them, including Jesus's mother and brothers. Together, they prayed, and they waited.

They knew that the Holy Spirit was coming. Jesus had said so Himself. And when the Holy Spirit arrived, He would give them power to go and make disciples of all nations.

But until then, they had to wait.

WHO DO YOU WANT TO TELL ABOUT JESUS? TAKE A MOMENT AND PRAY FOR THAT PERSON.

THE PROMISED HELPER

The disciples waited and prayed in the upper room as Jesus had commanded. Before He had returned to the Father, Jesus told them of a Helper who would come to them after He was gone: the Holy Spirit would aid them in their mission to go and make disciples.

As they prayed, they heard the sound of a violent, rushing wind filling the whole house. They saw what looked like flames of fire resting on each of them. They were being filled with the Holy Spirit— just as Jesus said they would be! They began to speak in different languages through the power of the Spirit.

At that time, the Jews were celebrating Pentecost and had traveled to Jerusalem from every nation. A crowd gathered as they heard the sound of the disciples. The crowds were confused—how could it be that they could all hear the disciples speaking in their own native languages?

Some of the people thought the disciples were drunk, but Peter stood up and spoke.

What's happening is what was spoken through the prophet Joel: "And it will be in the last days, says God, that I will pour out my Spirit on all people; then your sons and your daughters will prophesy, your young men will see visions, and your old men will dream dreams."

Listen to these words: Jesus of Nazareth was a man attested to you by God with miracles, wonders, and signs. Though He was delivered to die according to God's determined plan and foreknowledge, you used lawless people to nail him to a cross and kill Him. But God raised Him up, ending the pains of death, because it was not possible for Him to be held by death.

God has raised Him from the dead. We have all seen Him! He has been exalted to the right hand of God, and He has poured out what you both see and hear—the Holy Spirit. Therefore, let all Israel know with certainty that God has made this Jesus, whom you crucified, both Lord and Messiah.

What should we do?

Repent and be baptized in the name of Jesus Christ for the forgiveness of your sins, and you will receive the gift of the Holy Spirit.

Peter preached powerfully that day, and those who accepted his message were baptized. About three thousand people were added to their number. They devoted themselves to the disciples' teaching, to the fellowship, to the breaking of bread, and to prayer. And everyone who saw what was happening was amazed, and God continued to add to their number each day.

As more were added to their number, the message of the gospel continued to spread. During the lifetime of the disciples the gospel reached Jerusalem, Judea, Samaria, and beyond into the Roman Empire.

After the disciples died, the next generation of Christians continued to share the message, proclaiming the good news wherever they went. The gospel continued to go out into all the world through every generation until, finally, it reached us.

And now we are called to share this good news, in the same spirit and the same power as the first believers. Because the Holy Spirit who dwelt with the first disciples is the same Spirit dwelling within all who believe today. The Spirit continues to help us just as He did the first believers, teaching us to obey what Jesus commanded, and equipping us to share the message that has been entrusted to us—the call to repent and believe in the name of Jesus.

HOW HAVE YOU SEEN THE HOLY SPIRIT AT WORK IN YOUR LIFE?

THE POWER OF GOD AT WORK

In the early days of the church, Jesus's followers became known for their love for one another. They shared all they had with one another. They worshiped together in the temple each day and were devoted to the disciples' teaching. They ate in one another's houses with joy in their hearts. Many people throughout Jerusalem were in awe as they saw the signs and wonders—*miracles*—performed through the disciples.

> By faith in his name, his name has made this man strong, whom you see and know. So the faith that comes through Jesus has given him this perfect health in front of all of you.

One day as they were going to pray at the temple, Peter and John, two of Jesus's closest followers, met a man who could not walk. The man asked them for money, but Peter didn't have any. Instead, he said, "In the name of Jesus, get up and walk!" Immediately the man did, and all who saw what happened were in awe.

But not everyone was happy about what Jesus's followers were doing. The Jewish religious leaders—the high priest, the Pharisees and the Sadducees—held the disciples in contempt. They did not believe Jesus was the Messiah and were frustrated by the disciples' teaching about Jesus's resurrection. When they saw that miracle and the crowd listening to Peter and John's preaching, the leaders had the two disciples arrested. They ordered Peter and John not to speak of Jesus again, but the disciples refused. "It is better to obey God than human authorities," they said.

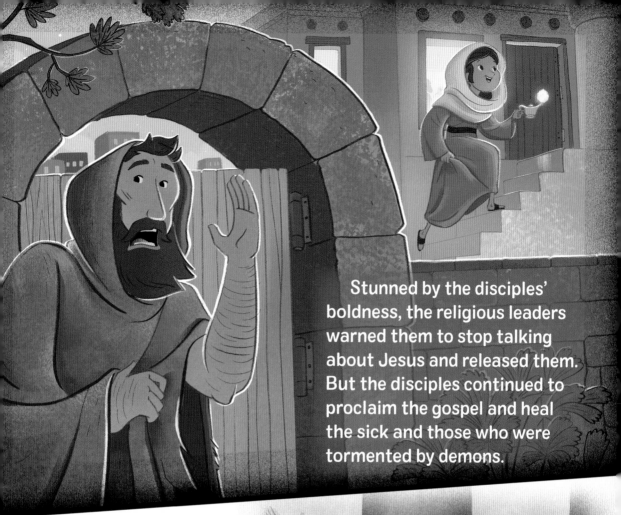

Stunned by the disciples' boldness, the religious leaders warned them to stop talking about Jesus and released them. But the disciples continued to proclaim the gospel and heal the sick and those who were tormented by demons.

Each day the religious leaders' contempt for the disciples grew. They would warn the disciples to stop speaking about Jesus, but the disciples wouldn't listen. The temple guards would beat the disciples, but they kept proclaiming Jesus's resurrection. The religious leaders would arrest the disciples, but the disciples would escape. It seemed as though there was nothing the religious leaders could do to make the disciples stop. *There has to be something we can do,* they thought. The group debated until Gamaliel, one of the most respected teachers among them, called for their attention.

Stay away from these men and leave them alone. For if this plan or this work is of human origin, it will fail; but if it is of God, you will not be able to overthrow them. YOU MAY EVEN BE FOUND FIGHTING AGAINST GOD.

The gospel continued to spread, and the disciples in Jerusalem increased. Even a large group of priests began to follow them!

Then, Stephen was killed.

Stephen was a servant in the church who distributed food to widows. He was filled with grace and the Holy Spirit and performed many signs and wonders in the sight of the Jews. But some opposed him as he shared the gospel, and they accused him of blasphemy.

"This man never stops speaking against this holy place and the law," they said. "For we heard him say that this Jesus of Nazareth will destroy this place and change the customs that Moses handed down to us!"

Stephen then told them their own history, how from the very beginning Israel had rebelled against God.

Look, I see the heavens opened and the Son of Man standing at the right hand of God!

Furious, the crowd picked up stones and began to throw them at Stephen. They yelled as loud as they could to drown out his voice and rushed toward him, continuing to throw stones at him. And then, his voice stopped. Stephen was dead. They had killed him.

Among the crowd was a man named Saul, a student of Gamaliel. He led the persecution of the church, and all except the disciples were forced to flee from Jerusalem. The disciples scattered throughout Judea and Samaria, mourning for Stephen as they went and hoping to evade Saul, who went from house to house dragging off men and women and putting them in prison.

This could have been the end for the church, but it was only the beginning. As the disciples scattered, they began to tell others of what had happened in Jerusalem, sharing the gospel with them. The message spread from Jerusalem and beyond into Judea, and from there to Antioch and Alexandria, Samaria and Caesarea. It even spread into Ethiopia when Philip met a servant who wanted to understand the prophecies of Isaiah.

Gamaliel was right: if the work of the disciples was of human origin, it would fail. It had to.

But it didn't.

Despite the opposition of the religious leaders and Saul ravaging the church, nothing could stop the spread of the gospel. It was the work of God, His plan from the very beginning to rescue and redeem sinners from every nation and people group.

And to prove it, He would call the church's greatest persecutor to become the gospel's greatest proclaimer.

HOW DOES THIS STORY ENCOURAGE US TO KEEP TELLING THE TRUTH ABOUT JESUS WHEN IT'S DIFFICULT?

FROM PERSECUTOR TO PROCLAIMER

Saul raced toward Damascus, his heart full of hatred for the disciples of Jesus. He had watched as Stephen was killed, and he'd approved. Soon after, he began a campaign to rid Judea of the Christians. *They were violating **God's Law**—calling Jesus of Nazareth "Lord," worshiping Him,* Paul thought. *Can't they see this is blasphemy? The Law is clear on the punishment for this sin:* **DEATH.**

Suddenly a bright light stopped Saul in his tracks. And a voice came from the light as he fell to the ground.

SAUL, SAUL, WHY ARE YOU PERSECUTING ME?

Who are You, Lord?

I AM JESUS, THE ONE YOU ARE PERSECUTING. BUT GET UP AND GO TO DAMASCUS AND WAIT.

The light disappeared, and Saul got up. But something was wrong—even though his eyes were open, he could not see. His companions, shocked by what they heard, took Saul by the hand and led him to Damascus.

Saul waited for three days and three nights. He did not eat or drink. His sight did not return.

And then, a man named Ananias arrived. He was a disciple of Jesus who lived in Damascus, one of the very same people Saul had come to arrest and put to death.

Brother Saul, the Lord Jesus, who appeared to you on the road you were traveling, has sent me so that you may regain your sight and be filled with the Holy Spirit.

Ananias prayed for Saul, and immediately something that looked like scales fell from Saul's eyes. He could see. But this wasn't just his normal vision—he could see Jesus for who He really was—the Lord, God Himself!

Saul got up and was baptized immediately. Then he stayed in Damascus for a long time, joining with the other believers and proclaiming the gospel.

In the synagogues, he told the Jews that Jesus of Nazareth was the Messiah, the Son of God, and everyone who heard him was amazed. How could it be that the same man who had been persecuting the followers of Jesus was now one of them? The longer he stayed, the stronger in the faith he became, and the more dangerous it was for him to stay. He kept confounding the Jews by proving that Jesus was the Messiah. They became angry and plotted to kill him. But this was not the end God had in mind for Saul.

Saul, also known as Paul, would suffer greatly for the sake of the gospel. He would be forced to flee from Damascus, but other believers feared him, and Jews in Jerusalem plotted to end his life. Over the next several years, he would continually face threats, imprisonment, and persecution. But he considered it all a mere inconvenience—a momentary affliction in comparison to the glory of Christ. He had been blind to the truth for so long, and now his only desire was for everyone to see the truth about Jesus.

His desire is the same desire that the Holy Spirit gives to everyone who believes—a desire for more and more people to see Jesus for who He is: the Son of God, the Messiah, the promised Rescuer who will make right everything that has gone wrong.

HOW DOES THE HOPE PROVIDED BY THE GOSPEL ENCOURAGE US NOT TO GIVE UP IN DIFFICULT TIMES OF LIFE?

PREACHING WHERE CHRIST HAS NOT BEEN NAMED

Paul had been in Antioch, a large city in Syria where the first Gentile church was, for about a year when the Holy Spirit called for him and Barnabas, another faithful teacher in the church, to go out into the world and share the gospel. The Antioch church prayed for them, and then the two men departed on the first of Paul's missionary journeys. On each journey, Paul and his ministry partners visited several cities throughout the Mediterranean region, traveling from Syria to cities in Asia, Greece, and eventually Italy to preach Christ where He had not yet been named.

During his first journey with Barnabas, Paul traveled to Cyprus, preaching in synagogues to the Jews. Then in Pisidia, many were amazed as Paul explained how the Scriptures revealed that Jesus was the Messiah. Some believed the message and became Christians. But the religious leaders began to insult Paul and Barnabas and drove them out of the synagogue.

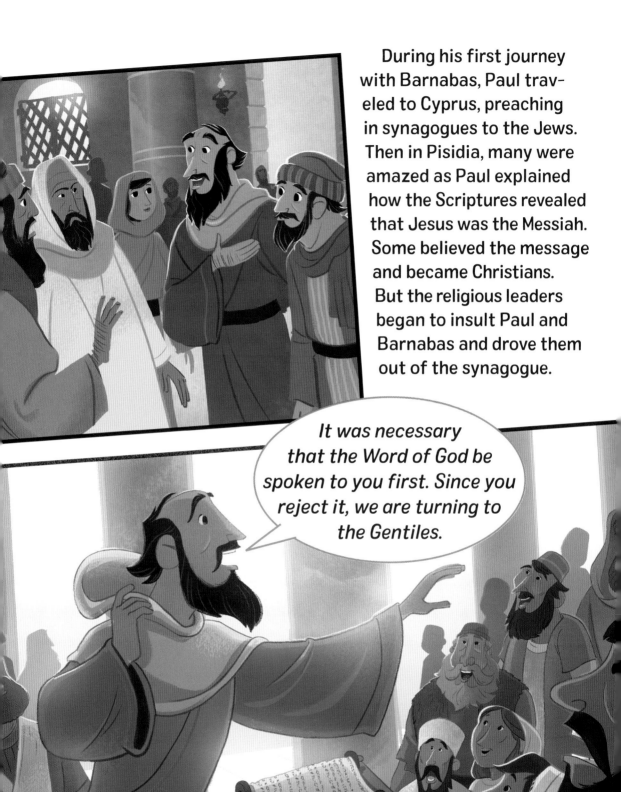

It was necessary that the Word of God be spoken to you first. Since you reject it, we are turning to the Gentiles.

Gentiles, the non Jewish people of the region, heard the gospel, something incredible happened: they believed, and the gospel spread through the whole region. But as it did, the Jews again stirred up crowds to persecute Paul and Barnabas and drove them away.

In Iconium they had a similar experience: when they preached about Christ, they were driven from the synagogues. But they found favor among the Gentiles, and many came to faith as a result. Paul and Barnabas left, but crowds of angry Jews began to follow after them.

When the missionaries arrived in Lystra, Paul and Barnabas were mistaken for gods after healing a man. Paul was shocked and tried to correct the crowd.

Why are you doing these things? We are people also, just like you, and we are proclaiming good news to you!

Paul then shared the gospel with the Gentiles, and many believed in Jesus. But before long, the crowds of Jews who had followed the missionaries from Iconium arrived.

They turned the crowds against Paul, and the people tried to kill him by stoning him—the same thing that had happened to Stephen in Jerusalem years before. When the crowd believed Paul was dead, they dragged his body outside the city. Then Paul got up and met Barnabas, who had somehow escaped being stoned himself, on the way to the city of Derbe.

As their journey came to an end, Paul and Barnabas returned to Antioch, stopping to encourage new believers in every community they visited at the beginning of the journey. When Paul and Barnabas returned to Antioch, they shared what God had done through them on the journey. The church rejoiced and praised God: the gospel was going out into the nations, just as Jesus commanded.

On his next journey, Paul traveled to Macedonia and met a woman named Lydia, whose entire household believed after hearing the good news of the gospel. A prison guard and his entire family also believed after Paul shared the gospel with him while Paul was under arrest!

In Thessalonica, Berea, Athens, and Corinth, even more Gentiles believed as Paul proclaimed Christ. But Paul was also met with resistance and threats in every city, from both Jews and Gentiles.

In Ephesus, a Gentile silver-smith started a riot because the Ephesians were no longer buying idols. In Greece, Jews plotted to kill Paul. In Corinth, the Jews put him on trial, accusing him of per-suading people to worship God in a way contrary to His Law.

What you worship in ignorance, this I proclaim to you. The God who made the world and everything in it—He is Lord of heaven and earth—does not live in shrines made by hands.

During his third journey, Paul encouraged many believers in Galatia, Philippi, and Asia before staying in Ephesus for three years. Then, when it was time to celebrate Pentecost, Paul set out to go to Jerusalem. Prophets came to warn him that he would be arrested, and friends tried to stop him. But Paul was determined to go to Jerusalem. He knew he would be arrested, and maybe even killed, but he couldn't not go. By going to Jerusalem, Paul would be able to preach Christ where He had not yet been named: in the throne room of the Roman emperor himself.

When Paul arrived at the tem-ple, a riot broke out when Jews from Asia—many of the same ones who had persecuted Paul before—saw him. The people began to beat him but stopped as soon as Roman soldiers arrived.

Paul's hands were bound in chains, and the soldiers asked Paul what was happening. The crowd shouted over Paul, so the soldiers carried him away to their barracks to listen to him. The crowd followed.

At their barracks, Paul asked to speak to the crowd. He shared how he was a Jew born in Tarsus and had once been a persecutor of the Christians. But then Jesus had appeared to him and changed his heart. When Paul shared how God planned to send him to the Gentiles, the crowd became furious.

"He should not be allowed to live!" they shouted. The soldiers prepared to flog Paul to learn the truth of what was going on.

But Paul asked, "Is it lawful for you to do this to a Roman citizen who is uncondemned?"

The soldiers stopped; if Paul was a Roman citizen, they couldn't beat or whip him if he were uncondemned. If they did, the soldiers would face serious charges—maybe even be flogged themselves! They unbound Paul's hands, and he asked to meet with the chief priests and religious leaders—the Sanhedrin.

While in custody, another plot to end his life began, and Paul was taken to Caesarea to stand before the Roman governor Festus and King Agrippa.

I stand on trial because of the hope in what God promised to our ancestors, the promise our twelve tribes hope to reach as they earnestly serve him night and day. I am being accused because of this hope. Why do any of you consider it incredible that God raises the dead?

Paul could not convince either Festus or King Agrippa of the truth, so he appealed to Caesar, asking that the emperor hear him. Festus agreed and put Paul on a ship to Rome.

As they sailed, a storm tossed the ship. But after the storm, a shipwreck, a snake bite, and many other difficulties, Paul arrived in Rome.

He remained in Rome for several years under house arrest as he waited to speak to Caesar. During that time he spoke with many believers who came to visit him and wrote letters to many others, including to the churches he had planted during his journeys.

His letters would encourage and inspire the churches to continue the mission that drove him: to preach Christ where He had not yet been named. To see others live from the same hope he had—the hope that God's promises to his ancestors would be and are being fulfilled in Jesus, the Son of God, the Rescuer who would save all who believe from their sins.

WHAT STOPS YOU FROM SHARING THE GOSPEL WITH OTHERS? HOW CAN PAUL'S STORY ENCOURAGE YOU?

LETTERS TO GOD'S PEOPLE

The early church was in danger, not just from its enemies, but from itself. The believers had many questions as they tried to make sense of what it meant to follow Jesus. What should they really believe about Jesus? What did it mean to have a new life in Him, when all their temptations and sins were still there? How could they face the spiritual threats that surrounded them?

Were Jewish and Gentile believers really the same? Was Jesus really going to make all things new? These questions only grew when other teachers began to tell them what it "really" meant to follow Jesus—and that way seemed different from what the disciples taught. To answer these challenges to the faith, the disciples and other church leaders began to write letters to remind the church of the truth of the gospel.

To a group of Jewish believers, one unknown writer explained the religious system that Jesus came to complete and how Jesus is better than spiritual beings. He is superior to the angels because He is their Creator, and He is the greater High Priest who did not need to offer a sacrifice for Himself. His is the perfect sacrifice that cannot be repeated, and He is the rest the Sabbath offers a taste of. "Jesus is the One God promised," the writer explained, "Hold onto your hope in Him with confidence."

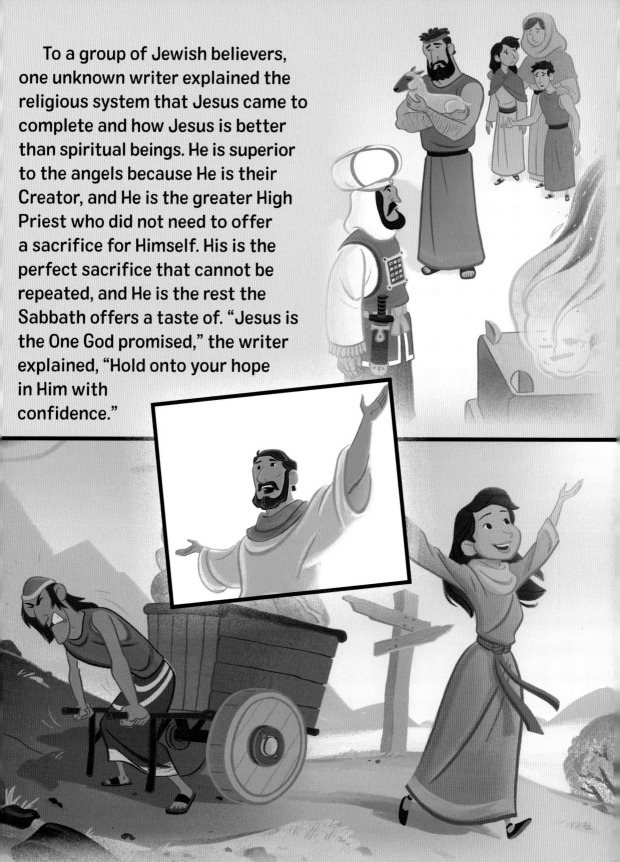

When false teachers tried to convince the Galatian church that they needed to obey the Law to be right with God, Paul encouraged the Galatians to hold fast to the gospel they first believed. Any other gospel was no gospel at all! "Christ set us free," Paul wrote. "Stand firm and don't become trapped by what can't save you."

Peter wrote to encourage believers to live godly lives in an unbelieving world. His encouragement included a challenge to willingly obey the human authorities who were persecuting the believers because of their faith in Christ. "Live in such a way that people will see your good works and glorify God," he wrote. "Honor everyone. Love your brothers and sisters in Christ. Fear God, and respect the emperor."

When the Corinthians formed factions around the teachers they followed—whether Apollos, Paul, or even Jesus Himself—and were divided by disagreements over spiritual gifts, Paul wrote to remind them that they were united in Christ. The gospel brought them together, and the gospel would keep them together.

John wrote a letter to remind believers that they were in the last days, and that in this time many false teachers would rise up to attempt to lead them away from the truth. But if they were children of God, they would not be deceived by those who denied Christ. The one who denies the Son is not

from the Father. Salvation comes only from faith in Jesus; those who love God obey Him. "Everyone who loves God loves His children," John wrote. "And this is how we love God: by obeying His commands."

When the Thessalonian church began to fear that they had missed Christ's return, Paul wrote to encourage them not to be upset or troubled. Before He would return, one called the man of lawlessness would be revealed. But Jesus would destroy this false god when He returned. Rather than worry, they were to watch and wait, living faithfully as they did.

Jude wrote to encourage another group of believers to contend for the faith against the false teachers who had crept into their fellowship. False teachers had always existed and would continue to exist until the day the Lord returned. But he encouraged these believers to continue to grow in their knowledge of the Christian faith and persevere in prayer as they waited for Jesus to return.

The disciples wrote their letters to guide the believers in the early church. They wanted them to remember God's truth and to live faithfully; to stand firm on the truth of the gospel and to pass that truth on to others. Through the centuries, the disciples have continued to teach the church through these letters, which still teach us what it means to follow Jesus. They remind us that we are free from the demands of the Law—that Christ has set us free to love and obey Him.

And these letters still give us hope, even as we wait for the day of the Lord to come, when all things will finally be made new.

Until that day, we are called to work as the early church was called to work, to keep ourselves in the love of God, full of confidence that Christ is able to keep us from stumbling.

WHY IS IT IMPORTANT TO BE CONFIDENT THAT CHRIST CAN KEEP US FROM STUMBLING? HOW DOES THIS HELP US LIVE FAITHFULLY?

THE END OF THE BEGINNING

John was an old man. It had been many years since he had first walked with Jesus, learned from Him, and been sent out to proclaim the good news. Now, he was the last of the disciples. The others had faced persecution and lost their lives for the sake of the gospel. John had faced many hardships and experienced much pain, but still he lived.

Suddenly, he had a vision:

Among seven lampstands, he saw a man dressed in brilliant white clothing, with eyes like lightning, hair as white as snow, and a gold sash around his chest.

It was Jesus, the First and the Last, and the Living One. He commanded John to write down what he was about to see and hear to share with the churches.

John was told to write seven letters to seven churches—encouragements and warnings to those who remained faithful to the truth but had lost their love for one another, allowed false teaching among them, and held fast in the face of terrible trials and suffering. But to the ones who conquered, Jesus would give blessing and honor.

And then the scene changed, and John was in a heavenly court, watching as the One on the throne held a scroll with seven seals. He waited for the One who was worthy to break the seal.

It was the Lamb, Jesus, the One who was dead and now lives. John watched as He opened each seal and as all of heaven gave Him honor and praise.

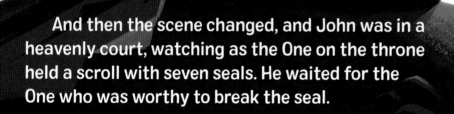

WORTHY IS THE LAMB WHO WAS SLAUGHTERED TO RECEIVE POWER AND RICHES AND WISDOM AND STRENGTH AND HONOR AND GLORY AND BLESSING!

John saw visions of terrible persecution, of beasts and a great dragon—the serpent from the Garden of Eden who tempted the first people—and a warrior on a white horse riding into battle, the King of kings and Lord of lords. He saw the dragon defeated and thrown into the lake of fire.

315

And then John saw people: a great multitude from every nation, every color, every ethnicity, and every language, from all times and places. With one voice they gave praise to Jesus. And Jesus went to each person and wiped every tear from every eye.

And all the people lived with Him in a heavenly city that descended to the earth, where sadness, sickness, sin, and death were no more.

And in the center of the city was a tree—the tree of life that bore fruit every month. The tree God planted in the garden in the beginning.

All were welcome to eat the fruit of this tree and enjoy life in the presence of God forever and ever, as God had intended from the beginning.

As the vision ended, Jesus said to John, "Look, I am coming soon!"

And John was filled with joy as he wrote these words down for all God's people throughout history, words that give us hope and confidence while we wait.

We know the end of the *beginning* of this story. But it is a story that has no end . . . only a promise that all who believe in Jesus—the One promised from the beginning—will enjoy life with Him forever. The One who is:

THE LAMB WHO WAS SLAIN, THE MESSIAH, THE KING OF KINGS, THE SON OF DAVID, THE SON OF ABRAHAM, THE SON OF ADAM, THE SON OF GOD.

He is coming soon. And while we wait, we say "Amen! Come, Lord Jesus!"

JESUS HAS ALREADY DEFEATED SIN FOREVER. HOW DOES KNOWING THIS GIVE YOU HOPE AS YOU FIGHT SIN RIGHT NOW?

REMEMBER:

Then beginning with Moses and all the Prophets, he interpreted for them the things concerning himself in all the Scriptures.—Luke 24:27

READ:

Read John 5:39–40. It's easy to read the Bible as if it were merely a list of rules and examples for us to follow, but this way of reading the Bible can leave us frustrated and confused. No matter how hard we try, we can't live up to all the examples, and we know we can't follow God's rules perfectly, which is why God wants us to see something bigger and more amazing. When we come to the Bible, He wants us to see Jesus as the hero of the story.

From Genesis to Revelation, the Bible tells one big story of God's plan to rescue and redeem the whole world through the life, death, and resurrection of Jesus. When we understand the Bible in this way, we see that it has nothing but good news for us because Jesus is the one all the examples point to. Jesus obeyed God perfectly for us, and when we trust in Him, Jesus gives us the Holy Spirit to help us obey God and make us more like Him every day.

THINK:

1. How would you summarize the Bible's big story?

2. Think about your favorite character in the Bible. Why is that person your favorite, and how does he or she point you to Jesus?

3. God says that we love Him by loving one another in our words and actions (Matthew 22:37–39). What are some ways you can love others this week?

4. It's hard to love others who aren't kind to us, but Jesus told us to pray for our enemies. Think of one person from school who you don't like, and pray for him or her.

5. God wants us to share the gospel with others. Who do you know who doesn't know Jesus? Make a plan to share the gospel with him or her.